If You Can't Wholesale After This

If You Can't Wholesale After This

I'VE GOT NOTHING FOR YOU...

Todd M Fleming

© 2017 Todd M Fleming
All rights reserved.

ISBN: 1979137641
ISBN 13: 9781979137645

Table of Contents

Introduction ·xi
   Mindset · xxiv
   Your Network Is Your Net Worth · · · · · · · · · · · · · · · · · · xxv
   Auditing Your Network · xxvi
   Self-Awareness · xxix
   Emotional Intelligence · xxx
   Asking Better Questions Creates A Better Life · · · · · · xxxii
   Abundance vs. Scarcity · xxxiv
   You Attract What You Think and Feel About · · · · · · · · xxxvi
   You Need to Be Rich ·xxxvii
   Think Big! · xxxviii
   Why Real Estate? Why Now? · xli
   Cycle of Real Estate · xliii
   Wholesaling Guide · xliv
   Wholesaling · xliv
   Assignment of Contract · xlvi
   Double Closing · xlviii

Step One · 1
   Protecting Yourself and Your Partners · · · · · · · · · · · · · · · · 1
   Title Company/Closing Attorney · 2

This Book is For:
The frustrated person who is tired of living inside the rat race and is willing to get out of their comfort zone to become truly free.

Introduction

When I began my business career, I never thought I would be teaching others how to achieve financial freedom or begin their own real estate investment business from scratch. It's funny how life and the universe takes you and uses you for things that you could never have imagined while you were growing up or even one year ago.

My only care growing up was playing baseball for the rest of my life, and when I say "only care," I mean the game totally consumed me. I drank it, ate it, slept it, and breathed it. Baseball was life! Playing ball and living the dream of playing in the big leagues was literally the only thing that mattered in my life until I was 24 years old.

I grew up in a middle class family of four in northeastern Ohio. I watched my father work long hours five to seven days a week to provide for my family while my mom worked various different positions with multiple companies. This is usually when the author of the book says, "My childhood lacked a lot of things that I always craved, like love, attention, and money." Mine was quite the opposite. Looking back, my childhood was pretty much perfect in my eyes. I had incredible parents who supported everything I ever wanted to do with unwavering passion and faith. My father came home from those long hours at work to help me hone my skills on the ball field. I have one older brother who also played sports and, ironically enough, also became a business owner and entrepreneur in his own right. He has even helped me create the incredible business I now own called The Kingdom Real Estate. The mission of my company is to teach people how to become financially free and live the lives they have always dreamed possible. You can visit The Kingdom at www.TheKingdomRealEstate.com to check it out for yourself.

I couldn't be luckier when it comes to having a more supportive and appreciative family. I hit the genetic lottery when it comes to family life. I realize that others do not come from such a supportive and loving background. I understand that something one person takes for granted might be an exotic delicacy to someone else. I use this knowledge as energy now that I am in my late 20s and have a young son of my own. I think back to the times when my parents gave up everything else they had going on at the time to help my brother and I pursue our individual dreams. I have incredible role models in my life, and I wouldn't trade them for the world. I remember that whenever I had any idea or a dream (such as professional baseball), my parents would always say, "Do it now; don't wait!" I heard that so often that I believed that was life's mantra! With their support I was able to focus on the things I loved the most. I can't thank them enough for that now. I didn't realize at the time how great a lesson their words and actions were providing me. I don't know if they knew the magnitude of the lesson they were teaching me, either. . .well, maybe they did.

Fast forward to my college days when I majored in "eligibility." I had zero passion or energy for academics. I went to school solely to play baseball and take the next step towards going pro. I went to class only to earn enough credits to be eligible to play every season. Most people wouldn't recommend this tactic, but it was the right path for me, and I wouldn't change it for the world. I think more people should follow their passion, even if that passion happens to be playing a major sport wherein the likelihood of getting drafted and playing professionally is miniscule. You won't be happy in life unless you know you gave it your all. Don't ever let something slip past you and cause you to wonder *what if* for the rest of your life. That is a plague that attacks too many souls today.

Four short years later I graduated college with a bachelor's degree in sports and business management, the latter of which I never considered I would use. I was still staring at a future in baseball. My baseball career eventually came to an end, though; I never ended up making it to the professional ranks. This took a toll on my mind and emotions for a long time. Not for a single day had I ever doubted that I would make it to the big leagues somehow. Once I realized it wasn't going to happen, I had to figure out what I was going to do with my life. I had to figure out what other people do. I had to learn how to "fit in." I had to get a job.

Over the next few years I battled with the demons of "failure" and figuring out how to make ends meet. I had never before had a job. I had never before had to conform. I began to understand what the phrase "day in, day out" really meant. I woke up, went to work, came home, went to bed, and then repeated the process, looking forward to Friday and the weekend so I could blow everything I made on whatever I was going to do that weekend with friends. I felt miserable and depressed. Every day I asked myself, *Is this really it? Is this all life is after your dream dies?*

This isn't to say that I didn't have good times and meet some great people, but my mind was one-directional and shallow. I was solely focused on my own problems. In other words, the world revolved around me. I had no self-awareness and no education on life, just school books and baseball.

Life went on like this for a couple more years before I had an "aha" moment one day as I sat in my little 6 x 6 cubicle at my job. If you just cringed a little when reading the word "cubicle," know that I feel your pain. At the time, I was a broker for a Fortune 100 company and was primarily making outbound cold calls to drum up business and help people pay too much for our product that, in all honesty, wasn't very good in my personal opinion. We were just a branch of a much larger corporation, and we had A LOT to learn even to begin to be competitive in the space we were trying to occupy. Ever felt like this yourself? If you work in a traditional J.O.B (Just Over Broke), you may have similar feelings and experiences.

I was in this position for two years, and then one day I was sitting quietly wondering what had happened in my life. *How did I fall into this rat-race trap? How did someone as talented and skilled as I was fall into the same life as everyone else? How do I change? What did I do wrong? Does this go on forever? I can't do this forever!* That's when it hit me! THIS is my fault! I finally asked myself a GREAT question: How and why was I here? No one had put a gun to my head and said, "Go do that." I had a choice. My life was a choice. It wasn't my employer's fault that I struggled financially. It wasn't my employer's fault that I had no financial training and was stressed each and every day about how I could eat without looking at my checking account balance first. (Do you do that? If so, this book will help!) It was MY FAULT. It was all me!

This was the first bit of self-awareness and realization I ever had. It took my being in so much pain that I couldn't bear the thought of coming to work one more day and making one more phone call for me to have this epiphany. This was my breaking point. This was the turning point of my life. This was the day that I made a decision and told myself, *I am going to build something of my own that means something to me, or I'm going to die.* I didn't care anymore. I was no longer so fearful of what would happen if I failed. I just started doing things differently.

GREAT QUESTION: WHAT HAVE I DONE SO FAR TO GET TO WHERE I AM RIGHT NOW?

Immediately following this "spiritual awakening," I took an honest look at my life and began putting a plan in place. At the time I had a car that was worth more than anything I had ever owned. That car was also the worst financial decision I had ever made in my life. I was lucky, though; I had a lot of equity (value above the principal payment) in it, so I decided to sell the car and put some reserve money in my pocket–$20,000 to be exact. I still had no clue what do with this money, but I knew I felt rich and that I was moving in the right direction. I quit my job the following day. This may or may not have been the right time to quit, but I had convinced myself that I officially had some reserves set in place and could begin working for myself and making a change in my life. The only problem at this point was I was still asking myself what I was going to do. *Am I going to start a business? Am I going to get a better job?* My gut told me I was done working for someone else. Every time I got bored somewhere doing the same thing over and over and never learning anything new, I was the worst employee.

I dedicated the following two months to learning about myself. I decided that if I was going to learn how to support myself like a real adult, I needed to discover what it was I liked to do. I had to completely rewrite the employee mindset I had developed while working for someone else. During these two months I felt unemployed and worthless as opposed to being self-employed or on a personal journey. I knew I had one hobby that I had provided me with some occasional success. That skill was trading in the stock market. The stock market was fascinating to me. There were stories of great wealth and riches to be had literally over night. And how could you go wrong if you followed someone who has been successful and made the same trades that that person did? I decided this was where I would begin paving my path to riches and success.

I started by diving into training programs and paid-membership sites so that I could follow along in chat rooms and profit along with the "gurus." I quickly realized it didn't quite work as advertised. The trades that were posted had typically already been made, or moved so quickly that you would get in at a bad price and get out at a worse price. This resulted in losses and a lot of self-doubt. I traded for about six months before I pulled my money out of the markets to keep learning and quit losing.

This is when I began asking myself more questions. *How do I get more confidence? Where do I find a passion? Where do I learn a skill from someone who is already successful? How do I become successful? How do I become rich? Is there anything that most millionaires have in common?* Just asking these questions caused me to seek the answers to these questions. I bought my first-ever book that hadn't been a school requirement. I should say I bought my first-ever book because I had never finished a single book in my life, with the exception of a book I had to read in my 5th grade language arts class.

I didn't buy just one book. I bought many books. I went from never reading a book to reading three to four a week. I became obsessed with knowledge and learning about the rich. After reading books like *Rich Dad Poor Dad* by Robert Kiyosaki, *Think and Grow Rich* by Napoleon Hill, and *Third Circle Theory* by Pejman Ghadimi, I realized that becoming rich and successful was a state of mind. It all starts with your mind. That's what all these guys had in common. Great, wealthy minds! They came from all sorts of different backgrounds and had childhoods way tougher than mine, so I knew it was possible. I just needed to learn how to apply this to my life.

Thus began my second wave of investing and trading in the stock market. I felt better. I felt strong. I felt confident. I knew I could be successful in the stock market. I joined a different chat room and gained some trading tips from people who taught specific patterns and what you could look for yourself instead of depending on the head guru to point out trades. The guru taught me how to find the trades before he ever made a move himself. This was my first taste of having a real mentor. This go around I was doing much better in the markets. I would have days of seven or eight successful trades, and I felt like it was just a matter of time before I hit it big and could retire forever and live the good life.

I was about eight months into my self-education endeavor when I saw that my living funds were dwindling. You would be amazed at how quickly $20,000 can leave your pockets when you are trading, deal. Oh, and it also cost $2,000. I returned home in disgust. I was once again defeated. I only had about $3,000 left to my name. If it cost $2,000 for the classes and would take two months to get my license, what was I going to survive on before I could make any money?

After thinking about it for a few days, I decided that I was going to do it no matter what, so I signed up for the classes using a credit card. I felt like a genius: buy now, pay later, and with all the money I was going to make after getting my license, I would be able to pay that card off in no time.

Fast forward three months–because two months turned out to be a bad estimate of how long the process would actually take. I finally had my license and could begin my real estate business. There was one slight problem: At this point I know nothing about real estate. I know people live in boxes, and some are nicer than others. I have no idea how to buy or sell these boxes, though. I have no clue about the process, so I began attending the broker's meetings and training sessions and shadowing other agents. I created my own little marketing campaigns, and I even picked up my first potential buyer. I was excited! I had clients who trusted me to represent them in a huge purchase, and I wanted to do the best job that I could. I began showing them houses and asking them to make offers, but they never did. Something was always wrong with each house. After a couple of months I was really starting to get desperate. My broker approached me and asked if I had paid my fees yet. I had no idea what she was talking about. As it turned out, the communication skills of the broker were poor, to say the least. I owed another $1,000!

The money was for the MLS (Multiple Listing Service) access and to cover miscellaneous fees the broker charged for using things like the copying machine and the desk they had assigned me. Are you kidding me? I didn't have $1,000. I was upset, so I asked if I could pay it out of my first commission check. She explained that was fine insofar as the broker charges were concerned, but noted that the house would need to have a big price tag to cover what I owed. The commission rate was 6%, but I wouldn't get all of that because the broker takes a big chunk of it. I was in shock and awe. This hadn't been explained to me–or if it had, I had overlooked it in my excitement of getting started in my new career. In actuality, I was just an employee again, but this time I had to pay to go to work!

That was the last time I entered that office. I couldn't bring myself to return after I felt like I had been lied to and betrayed. I then understood why some agents went through brokers like they were a revolving door. The turnover was terrible. But now I had this cloud of doubt hanging over me again. I was now close to being totally broke, and I had no real way of completing my first real estate deal with no leads in sight and no buyers looking to put in offers. This time I couldn't sit around and sulk, though. I had to make progress; otherwise, I didn't know where my next meal was going to come from.

A few days later I came upon an interview with another real estate investor on my favorite entrepreneur website. This investor had been through the crash of '08 and had recovered from bankruptcy to become a millionaire again. He indicated that he did not have a real estate license himself and said that you didn't need a license or any money to invest in real estate. That intrigued me. How could this be possible? Real estate is the most expensive thing on the planet. How can you possibly buy it with no money? He talked about flipping houses with no cash out of pocket and mentioned that he had a free training webinar available. I signed up immediately and watched the entire training video over the next couple of hours. I was shocked. I was excited. I was mad at the broker for whom I had previously worked. I was upset that I had wasted so much time. Why would I ever work for someone else if I could do what this guy was talking about with no license and no money. Good thing, too, because I had no money. I hated the idea of splitting all of my profits with a broker who didn't even help me do the deal anyway. I was going to throw my license in the trash after all of that work and begin investing–NOW!

What was he talking about in the webinar training? He called it wholesaling. At the time I called it life-saving! He was telling me that I could make money in real estate in a few short weeks with no risk and no money out of my own pocket! Where do I sign up? How do I learn more? What do I need to do today to make this work? Do I need experience? I don't need a license? What do I do first? These are all great questions that I asked myself. Once again, as I asked myself these questions, I realized the answers to them would lead me to my first deal and my first paycheck in nearly a year! I dearly needed that paycheck. At this point things were REALLY tight. My girlfriend at the time (now wife) had even moved in and began helping out with bills and living expenses. You want to feel less like a real man? Depend on someone else to pay some of your most basic living expenses.

GREAT QUESTION: WHAT DO I HAVE TO DO RIGHT NOW TO MAKE THIS WORK FOR ME?

This is where we pause my story to begin training you for your first real estate deal. I completed my first real estate wholesale deal just a few weeks after watching the previously mentioned interview and training webinar. I completed the deal with only $11 in my checking account. Let me repeat that. I closed my first real estate wholesale deal with only $11 in my pocket! I was dead broke. I had no money for marketing. I had no money for networking. I had no money for closing costs. I didn't have enough for dinner, except for fast food.

You might be wondering why I provided so much detail on my hardships and struggle in the beginning. The reason is this: I understand where you are coming from. I understand how it feels to be broke. I understand how it feels when you're not able to provide for yourself, let alone someone else or a family. You MAY BE going through your own $11 moment right now. I understand how you feel, and I want you to know that this book will guide you through your first deal no matter what your situation is. This book will help you build a base of success and get you on the road to financial freedom. You will be able to look back at this moment and say, "When I read <u>If You Cant Wholesale After This: The I've Got Nothing For You!</u> I realized I could invest in real estate, no matter what." This will be the turning point.

I now mentor hundreds of students, many of whom have already completed their first deals and are scaling their businesses. They each started with no money. Many of these students have been able to move on from their regular 9-to-5 jobs and work on their real estate business full time now. Take what is in this book to heart and take action immediately. The only thing stopping you from reaching your dreams is your lack of action. Action is the most important thing in life. Knowledge is not power; *applied* knowledge is! You can read some of their stories in the back of me during my journey and continues to help me to this day. This was a huge motivation for my company, The Kingdom Real Estate. We meet every single day! When you become a family member within the Kingdom, you have 24/7 access to people who are on the same journey as you. Want a fantastic way to surround yourself with people you love and respect? Create your own community! I am going to speak more on this topic in a later section and teach you how to create different local and virtual get-togethers so that you can network with the best of the best and set yourself up for success!

GREAT QUESTION: WHAT DO THE LIVES OF MY FIVE CLOSEST FRIENDS LOOK LIKE?

Auditing Your Network

We all begin as products of our environment. As we start to grow and look at situations in a different light, we begin to understand that we can manipulate our environment to best suit us. We control who we hang out with. We control who we follow on social media. We control whose advice we take. Are you listening to someone who has done what you want to do? Are you listening to someone living the life you want to live? Are you hearing noise and negativity from those around you? These are some of the questions you should ask yourself in order to audit your network and your closest friends. If you don't like your answers to these questions, your answers will help you identify what you need to change. If you have never filtered out your social media accounts, I can guarantee that you see more negative than positive images and thoughts. This is poison for your mind. So, let's discuss how to correct this.

When you look at your social media accounts, such as Facebook, Instagram, Pinterest, Snapchat, and any others of that genre, what do you see? Do you see negativity? Do you watch the news religiously? I am going to let you in on a little secret. The news sells death, destruction, and negativity. They are SELLING you news. I am sure you have listened to or watched the news before and wondered if anything good in the world happened that day, or if it was just all garbage and terrorist attacks. The news media hand picks what to post and advertise. The first step in auditing yourself and others around you is to stop watching the news. If you feel you need to be informed, that's fine, but don't let the news consume you and rob you of your energy.

It is important to audit and filter your social media even more. You can just turn off the news and walk away. In contrast, we are always connected to social media these days, and many people log onto their accounts hundreds of times a day. Scroll through your timelines and pick out the negative comments, complaining, and whining. When you identify these posters, the best thing to do is to unfollow these posts and people. They will inhibit your growth and impede your mind.

You are being fed messages all day long, whether you are conscious of it or not, and a large majority of these messages are negative. If we don't counteract these negative messages and teachings with positive outlooks, we are doomed and will never be able to grow. Take the time to filter your accounts so you see only positive and uplifting posts. By the way, this isn't just a one-time thing. You need to monitor your social media accounts and eradicate the negativity on a regular basis. The good news is that after you do it once or twice, it becomes much less time consuming. And you will thank yourself for doing this almost immediately because you will feel better throughout the day without all the negativity surrounding you.

After auditing your friends and who you follow, you need to review your own accounts. This can be painful. You may notice that you have fallen into the same trap and been posting in negative tones and painting the wrong picture about yourself to others. But that's okay because we are now going to be changing this. Run through all of your prior posts and delete anything that you wouldn't want other positive people to see now. You might be amazed at how much you have changed over the years. I know that when I did this, I found it incredible to observe the growth that I've experienced in my life in just the past five years. Think about it: if you can actually see the growth over the last couple of years, imagine how much you can change and accomplish in the next 30 to 40 years!

Once you have filtered all of your own posts, look at the pictures that you have on your profile and remove any that don't scream SUCCESSFUL! If there are any pictures depicting drinking, partying, or other unprofessional activities, delete them and move on. We are rewiring our minds and rewriting our profiles, and it's important that the photos of us reflect this. You will soon have a lot of people checking on you to see if you are someone with whom they'd want to work and/or in whom they'd want to invest; you don't want to miss out on big opportunities because you got drunk in 2012.

These little audits will become a valuable habit and something to share with your fellow investors when the time comes. People respect others who respect themselves and hold themselves to a certain standard. These audits will serve as a great measuring stick as well. You will be able to observe the point at which you started your journey to freedom and success while others stayed the same. It's exciting for you and sad for others at the same time.

GREAT QUESTION: WHAT DOES MY SOCIAL MEDIA SAY ABOUT ME?

Self-Awareness

Self-awareness comes to those who expand on their knowledge and focus on learning and asking great questions. The ability to stop and examine a situation from different perspectives is essential in business and problem-solving. When you expand on what you already know, you begin to gain more insight on the views of others. You begin to realize that you are simply a piece in this world and not the center of the universe. Have you ever met someone who clearly believed the world revolved around them and that their problems were more important and drastic than those of everyone else? I'm sure you have; we all have!

When you lack self-awareness, you are extremely limited in being able to solve any real problems, including your own. People who believe they are the center of the universe never notice the abundance of opportunities around them because they see life and the universe through one filter and one filter only–their first child, to the nearest medical facility, and you were, in fact the cause of frustration because you were in the way of his getting the help they needed in time? Eye opening, isn't it? What if someone in that car was injured? What if the driver had a legitimate reason to get past you as quickly as possible?

Asking yourself these questions is an example of being self-aware and looking at a situation through another's lens. Once you begin practicing this, you will realize each day gets a little bit easier to navigate. Life itself starts to become less stressful and more fulfilling.

GREAT QUESTION: AM I THE CAUSE OF FRUSTRATION IN THIS SITUATION?

Asking Better Questions Creates A Better Life

You may have noticed a theme within this book so far. A great question to ask yourself is presented at the bottom of each section. If you study and ask yourself these questions daily, you will surely grow and become better at what you do. Asking yourself these questions will force you to seek answers and look at a problem from different perspectives for different types of solutions. You will become a master problem solver. The better the questions you ask, the better the answers and results you will get.

Questions are the basis of all successes and the core of every great idea. Before a great idea is born, a great question is asked. The question may be spoken aloud or simply mulled in someone's mind, but it is the seed for the idea. Nothing appears in the physical world before a question is posed and its solution sought by means of idea, planning, and execution. If you want to have great results and great big successes, you need to start asking better questions. Basic questions get quick, basic answers and will put a ceiling on your success and learning. When great questions are asked, brainstorming occurs, and brilliant ideas and solutions are created. If you want to live a great big life, ask great big questions for which you must find answers.

This concept can be observed in all successful companies. Think of Apple. The question was, "How can we make computing simple and available to everyone?" That's one hell of a question. That gave birth to the largest and most powerful company on the planet. Apple has more liquid capital than the American government. Think about that. Maybe your question should be, "How can I create something that affects so many people that I earn more liquid capital than the American government?" That's a pretty big question. That's a question that requires a lot of thought and effort to answer. Your goal really shouldn't just be monetary, though.

Want to know what question I asked myself when forming The Kingdom Real Estate? I asked myself the following: "How can I create a community in which people pick each other up and interact as a family so that everyone is committed to the same goal of getting everyone financially free? Where anyone can get any question answered at any time instead of just buying a course and being alone in the end?"

My Answer: www.TheKingdomRealEstate.com . Not just a real estate group. A Family.

GREAT QUESTION: HOW CAN I ASK BETTER QUESTIONS TO ADVANCE MY LIFE AND THE LIVES OF THE PEOPLE AROUND ME?

Abundance vs. Scarcity

Ask yourself the following questions: Is there enough money in the world to go around? Is there enough love to be shared always? Is there enough time in the day to do everything that I want? Is success and happiness attainable by all? Is there enough opportunity for everyone to capitalize on? If you answered "no" to any of these, I would strongly suggest you read this section multiple times before moving on. It will be essential for you to understand the abundance mindset versus the scarcity mindset that plagues so many individuals today. Remember, you are looking to change things in your life and change your future, so you need to start setting yourself apart from the "norm." You have managed to adapt to your current surroundings and mindset; it's now time to start molding yourself around a new, more exciting perception of life.

Let us first define abundance and scarcity. Abundance is having a large quantity of something. It is having more than enough and enough to share. An abundance mindset believes that there will always be enough resources available so that you never have to take advantage of someone else or take from others. You will always have the ability to share and grow. Scarcity is the idea that there is a limited amount of resources to go around; thus, one must manipulate and hurry to collect enough so that his resources don't run out. This causes stress and the constant worry that "there isn't enough."

The scarcity mindset limits potential and growth. It will ensure that you struggle to reach goals and limit your problem-solving ability. With a scarcity mindset you will struggle to see perspectives different from your own, and it will be difficult to see past your own struggles and hardships because, in your mind, the world will always be out to get you. There is never enough. You are never satisfied. The scarcity mindset isn't open to happiness, love, satisfaction, and different ideals.

The abundance mindset is quite the opposite. The abundance mind understands that there is enough opportunity for all. It takes pride in helping others, solving problems, seeing different views, learning, and sharing ideas. The person with an abundant mind sees the world from a different looking glass. That person sees potential. He/she sees all the surrounding opportunity and will allow himself/herself to capitalize on that opportunity at an incredible rate. Have you ever heard the saying, "Open your mind"? Truly believing that there is enough in this world will help change your perception of business and life. It will enable you to put others first and give more, and this will provide you with greater returns than you could have ever imagined possible previously. To relate this to getting your first real estate deal, it is essential that you keep an open mind and see the opportunity in each hardship. This will help you solve the problem of your seller. I will cover this in detail in the "Building Rapport" section of this book.

GREAT QUESTION: AM I THINKING ABOUT THIS PROBLEM WITH AN ABUNDANT MINDSET?

powerful "whys" that you can have. Everyone needs a "big why," a big reason to motivate them to advance to the next level. The ability to support my family and loved ones is one that always helps me through down times or times that I don't feel particularly energetic. Consistency is king! Lean on your big powerful why, and it will give you the energy to take the next step toward your dreams.

GREAT QUESTION: IF SOMETHING HAPPENED TO A LOVED ONE AND THEY COULD NO LONGER WORK, COULD I TAKE CARE OF AND SUPPORT THEM?

Think Big!

Thinking big is the best kept secret in business. Your limits are based only on how big you can think. I want you to think of some of the most successful people on the planet. You may have a slew of different people running through your mind right now. Professional athletes, business people, Steve Jobs from Apple, Bill Gates from Microsoft, Jeff Bezos from Amazon, actors, singers, and other entertainers are all great examples. All of these people have at least one thing in common. All of these people had the guts to dream and think BIG! You can only go as far as you think. If you are living for Friday and the weekend, this is a big reason why you are currently limited to that life. You need to start thinking bigger and setting bigger goals.

Did you know that it takes just as much energy to think big as it does to think small, or, the word I hate most in the English language, "realistically"? What is realistic anyway? Who came up with the idea that people should believe that they can only achieve what others already have? Who decided that thinking small and setting super-small goals that can be completed in a single day was a good idea? Who brainwashed the world into thinking that thinking big is reserved only for a select few people and that success is random? It is not random! Success starts with thinking big! I want you to start practicing this. I want you to start molding yourself into a big dreamer instead of being someone who looks forward to Saturday, and then dreads the thought of Sunday night. There is more to life than this, I promise. I think you know this, too, or else you wouldn't still be reading this book.

Here are some examples of how you might start thinking with great big potential instead of what's "realistic" to others:

"Realistic" Thinker: "I want to take my child skiing this winter."

Big Thinker: "I want to take my child and his entire school skiing this winter."

"Realistic" Thinker: "I want to enable my wife to retire so she can stay home with the kids."

Big Thinker: "I am going to enable my entire family and close group of friends to retire so we can all work on our life's passions together!"

"Realistic" Thinker: "I am excited to spend a week's vacation on the beaches of South Carolina."

Big Thinker: "I am excited to take a 2-month trip to Bali and explore the different beaches and culture!"

"Realistic" Thinker: "I want to make $50,000 per year."

Big Thinker: "I am going to make millions of dollars per year so I can give back and help more than others."

Which type of thinker do you believe lives the bigger life? Who do you think lives the better life? It may be uncomfortable at first to start thinking big. It will take some practice because we have been taught all our lives to think and act small so that we don't get hurt. Stop worrying about getting hurt and failing. Failing is a sign of learning. Failing is a sign of growth. Successful people fail their way to the top. If we don't fail at things, it means we aren't growing. It means we aren't trying new things, and we aren't trying to get to the next level.

The concern over failure actually doesn't stem from a fear of being hurt or bad at something. It stems from the social want and need to be accepted. We don't want to look stupid. We don't want to look bad in front of our friends. We don't want them to think less of us. We are more afraid of what others think than achieving something we are actually capable of doing. A mentor of mine once told me something I always keep in mind. It was this: You can't look good and learn at the same time. Anytime that I am trying something new I remind myself of this and remind myself that whatever I might be scared of right now is a great sign that I should be doing that one thing because it is what will get me to the next level in my business and in my life. I encourage you to adopt this mindset and way of thinking. You won't regret it. You will thank yourself many times over and show others what is possible with the opportunity around you. You will continuously complete new goals and achieve new heights. Instead of thinking less of you, everyone will be thinking, "How do I do that?"

Let me end this section by providing you with a simple rule to follow to determine if you are thinking big or not in the situation you are currently facing:

If someone else has or had the same idea as you, You are NOT thinking big enough!

GREAT QUESTION: HOW CAN I THINK BIGGER IN EVERY ASPECT OF MY LIFE IN ORDER TO IMPROVE NOT ONLY MY LIFE BUT THE LIVES OF EVERYONE AROUND ME?

Why Real Estate? Why Now?

Once you have built a base mindset and a core from which you will be able to pull energy and positivity, it is time to apply this in your real estate business. You need to start with mindset because without a strong mind, you will be apt to run and quit when things get tough. It is essential that you don't quit! I can promise that if you don't quit and you follow the steps laid out in this book, you will close your first deal and make your first dollar in real estate. I can say that with 100% confidence. If you want to be successful in real estate and investing, you must forever banish from your mind the thought of ever quitting when things get tough. Use the tools and techniques presented in the sections of this book to keep your mind strong. If you need help and want to surround yourself with more people like yourself, visit www.thekingdomrealestate.com, and you will find a family that will surround you and lift you up in times of need until you can lift others up yourself.

as you begin. Your network and buying partners will take care of this for you.

GREAT QUESTION: AM I LEVERAGING MY NETWORK TO LEARN AND ADAPT AS QUICKLY AS I NEED TO?

Wholesaling Guide

Follow These Next Steps To Complete Your First Deal In Real Estate In As Little As A Couple Of Weeks

Wholesaling

Wholesaling. What is it? How do I do it? What's its potential? Why should I start here? Is it risky? Is it common? Is it legal? How much money do I need? Does it take a long time? Is it hard? Should I be as scared as I am? I live in a small town; does it work here? I live in a big expensive market; does it still work here? Do I need a real estate license to do this? Can I do this with a partner? How long does this take to learn? Do I need to quit my job to start? Can I do this part time? What if real estate goes away?

I am going to cover all of these questions and more as I discuss the nine steps to your first real estate deal, with no money out of pocket. But first things first. Let me explain what wholesaling is and why it is so brilliant.

Wholesaling, in its simplest form, is the art of selling your interest in purchasing a property to another buyer for a fee. You flip houses that you don't even own! You see, when you approach someone and sign a purchase agreement (contract) for his or her house, that person is legally bound to sell that property to you and can no longer sell it to someone else. This is your interest in the property. You now have the ability at this point to sell your interest in that property for a fee to someone else if you would like. This is a wholesale transaction. You put a property under contract (i.e., you sign a purchase agreement with a seller) for a lower price and sell the contract for more than that agreed-upon price for a profit. The seller gets paid what you agreed to pay him for the house, and then the buyer pays you the difference. Let me give you a concrete example of how this transaction is executed before moving on to the exact steps to take to make this happen.

Example 1: You offer to pay a seller $100,000 for his property. The seller agrees. You sign a purchase agreement for $100,000. Before closing on the property, you have a buyer who wants to buy that property and contract from you for $130,000. You sell your contract to that buyer for $130,000. The original seller gets the agreed upon $100,000, and you walk away with the remaining $30,000. You just made $30,000 and never took a single dime out of your pocket. I will also teach you how to make this transaction risk free such that you close every contract you have, and everyone is happy every time–seller, buyer, and yourself alike.

There are two common ways to complete this transaction. You can assign the contract (sell the contract), or you can do what is called a double closing. I will explain the difference between the two next.

GREAT QUESTION: IF IT DOESN'T TAKE MONEY TO MAKE MONEY, HOW BIG OF A DEAL CAN I FACILITATE TO CHANGE MY LIFE?

Assignment of Contract

Assignment of contract is just a fancy term for selling your original purchase agreement contract to an end buyer for a fee. This is the cleanest and simplest way to complete a wholesale transaction. It requires top-notch communication between you, the seller, and the end buyer as well as with the title company/closing attorney, but it is the preferred way of doing business in most cases. The steps below summarize the process for an assignment of contract:

1. Original seller agrees to sell house to you for a specified price.
2. You sign purchase agreement contract with seller that states that the contract is "assignable."
3. You take that contract to a buyer you have found who buys that contract from you for a fee.
4. You contact the original seller and have him sign an "assignment of contract" form that explains you have a partner who will be stepping in to close on the property in your place and that you will be receiving a fee for your service from the end buyer and that the original seller will receive the exact dollar amount specified in the original contract and that nothing changes on his end.
5. The original seller goes to closing, and the end buyer goes to closing.

6. After closing, the title company sends the original seller the money agreed to in the original purchase contract with you. The title company cuts you a check for the assignment fee agreed upon by you and your end buyer. The end buyer gets title to the property.

In an assignment of contract everyone is notified and understands what the process is. Everyone signs off on everyone's numbers, profit, and prices. This is important to note. When assigning a contract you need to have both the seller and end buyer sign an assignment sheet that stipulates the details of the transaction. There is no new purchase agreement between you and the end buyer. The end buyer is simply assuming all the responsibilities stated in your original contract with the seller. This means it is important to lay out good terms that will work for your end buyer. Once the original contract is signed and agreed upon, you can't change things at or after closing. For example, if your end buyer isn't willing to pay all the closing costs, don't tell the seller that all closing costs will be paid by the buyer. Make sure all parties know the precise details of the transaction so that there aren't any surprises when they get to the closing.

Assigning contracts is a great way to solve problems, build capital, and build momentum in your real estate business. There are no closing costs that you, the wholesaler, must pay under an assignment. All closing fees are paid by the seller and/or your end buyer. You don't even have to go to closing to get the deal done. Once everyone has signed off on the assignment sheet, you simply wait for closing and your check. In a later section I will discuss what you should expect and what you should be communicating to both your seller and buyer while waiting for closing.

4. You show property to buyer by means of pictures, video, or a walkthrough.
5. You agree to a sell the property to the buyer at a price that is higher than your purchase price with seller.
6. You sign purchase agreement between you and the end buyer.
7. You now have two sets of contracts: one between you and the seller, and one between you and the buyer.
8. Next, you send the two sets of contracts to the title company or closing attorney and let them know that you plan to close on the first contract and then immediately resell and close on the second contract either same day or next day.
9. At this point you are waiting for closing while the title company performs their due diligence and prepares new deeds for you and your buyer.
10. Everyone is alerted to a closing date by the title company.
11. First, you close to purchase the property from the seller. You sign with the seller first.
12. Next, after signing to purchase the property, you will sign to sell the property to your end buyer.
13. At this point you have signed closing docs for the purchase and the sale.
14. You pass your funds to close the first deal to the title company, and they file that piece of the transaction. You officially own the property now.
15. Immediately following this, your end buyer passes along the funds to purchase the property from you to the title company, and the title group files the sale. The end buyer now owns the property.
16. Finally, the title group disperses funds to everyone, and you will have your profit after paying the required closings costs.

As you can see, the A-B-C transaction is much more complicated and takes twice as much work. You may also be thinking, "Hey, you promised it wouldn't take any money to close my first deal!" It's true that this method takes capital in order to close the first portion of the deal. Luckily, it doesn't need to be your capital. There are lenders all over the country who engage in what is called transactional funding. Transactional funding is a type of lending arrangement specifically designed to enable real estate wholesalers to purchase a property without using his or her own funds. So, don't worry; you can still complete deals like this even if you don't have any money of your own right now.

Remember to take the cost of this transactional funding into account, though, when structuring your deal. You will have to pay a fee to the lender to cover the costs of the paperwork and the short-term loan. This is just the cost of doing business, and the fee is typically deducted from your profit after the deal has been completely finalized, so you needn't fork out any money up front. Nevertheless, this is something you need to be aware of when you are making and accepting offers if you plan to double close. You need to make sure you have a large enough spread (the difference between the price you pay for the property and the price you sell it for). When establishing your spread, take all closing costs and funding into account. If you have a small spread and big fees to cover, you may end up losing money on the deal. You will also want to be aware of taxes, and bear in mind that your name will be on the chain of title for that property forever from that point on.

You may be wondering why in the world you would ever think about using a double closing when assignments are so simple; however, there are occasions in which a double closing is beneficial. Some people recommend using a double closing when your spread is larger so that your clients (sellers and buyers) don't get uncomfortable with how much you are making on the deal. When you double close, no one has to sign off on your profits, and neither the seller nor the buyer know what your contract prices are for the opposite parties.

I mention this only to inform you about the process and the possibilities that it holds. My moral compass is such that I don't believe in hiding what I am making on the deal. Remember that you are providing value to the sellers and the buyers alike when you structure these deals. If you focus on the problem solving and services that you are providing, there should be no need to hide what you are making. I personally never look to hide anything about my business, including my profits. This helps build transparency and a good reputation. Honestly speaking, if you are dealing with a buyer who thinks you shouldn't be paid for your services, that person isn't a good partner anyway.

But I understand that there are people out there who think only they should get paid, and this is a way to avoid that pain. At this point I like to disclose that I have seen assignment contracts signed off on for hundreds of thousands of dollars, so it really comes down to your communication with and the size of the problem that you are solving for your seller. If you have earned your payment through an honest, ethical, and transparent business transaction, you have absolutely nothing to be ashamed of. I don't care how big the assignment fee is.

So, besides avoiding the occasional socio-economic pain, why else would you perform a double closing? It is sometimes preferred by certain title companies and attorneys. While assignments are perfectly legal, there are times when the title company would rather close two clean back-to back transactions. Double closings involve more work and more risk, so this is rare, but ultimately possible.

The most legitimate reason to double close as opposed to assigning the contract is if the original purchase agreement you have signed with your seller is "non-assignable." This also is rare, but there are times in which a seller will stipulate that the contract is non-assignable. This means that you cannot sell the contract; the contract allows only you to close on the property, personally fulfilling the duties agreed upon within the contract. This doesn't happen very often because the sellers aren't overly concerned about who is closing on the property. They are only concerned that you are solving their problem for them.

As you might expect in seeing all the extra steps involved in a double closing, it is important to be dealing with a title company that is experienced and knowledgeable in this type of transaction. If any of the steps are overlooked during this process or any of the closing documents are mishandled, it could spell disaster for title insurance or chain of title. Unfortunately, this is not as rare as the other issues I discussed above. With so many moving pieces and so many hands working the deal, details can be lost. Overall, this isn't something that you should be afraid of; just be aware and know to look for any red flags.

The number one rule in wholesaling–and real estate in general–is to be honest, ethical, and transparent. You are in this game to solve problems for sellers and buyers alike. You will be getting paid for the value that you bring to the marketplace. Never lie. Never cheat. Never bend the truth regarding anything in a contract. It will crush you and your business and can land you in serious trouble as well. If you follow this guide to a tee, you won't have to worry about any of that because you will be solving problems transaction(s) since this is the entity that will hold any deposit money that you or your end buyer must provide. My objective in making this the first step is to set you up for success and protect you from making any early mistakes, like giving the money to the wrong person. I wish someone had explained this to me when I was starting. Luckily, I never lost any money, but I very well could have in a few different situations where money changed hands outside of "escrow." **Escrow** is a term for a trusted third party, such as a title company or closing attorney, that holds any money involved in a transaction until certain specified conditions are met. This keeps you safe! So, please, never hand money to anyone other than the organization that is handling the closing. Now that we are clear on who the keeper of the money should be, let's get going on our first deal!

GREAT QUESTION: IS THE PERSON I AM HANDING MONEY TO TRUSTWORTHY AND CONNECTED WITH THE TITLE COMPANY/CLOSING ATTORNEY?

Title Company/Closing Attorney

The state you are living or working in may determine whether you use a title company or an attorney to close your real estate transactions. Some states require that an attorney be used to close the deal; others stipulate that a title company handle it; still others allow either a title company or an attorney to act as the closing agent. It doesn't make a difference whether you use a title company or a real estate attorney, however. The process is the same, and the questions you will be asking these people are identical in every scenario.

I personally use a title group, and they are fantastic. I love them! They are like family to me at this point. I know other investors who use an attorney to close their deals, and, guess what? They love their attorneys, too. You will be building strong relationships with these people to ensure you are both bringing great value to each other's business. I am going to teach you how to do this. Throughout the rest of this book, I will be using the terms "title company/title group," and "closing attorney" interchangeably, so just know the details I provide apply to both.

TITLE COMPANY: A company that completes all the paperwork for your transaction. This team will handle your closing documents, title searches, purchase agreements, money transfer, and state filing.

CLOSING ATTORNEY: A real estate attorney who completes all the paperwork and handles the closing, money transfer, title search, and state filings.

Notice how both perform identical functions? So, don't let the minor detail of which you should use affect you; it doesn't matter. Instead let's discuss how to find these new team members of ours.

GREAT QUESTION: DO I HAVE SOMEONE ON MY TEAM THAT I CAN DEPEND ON TO HANDLE ALL THE PAPERWORK AND LEGALITIES SO I DON'T HAVE TO?

Finding a Title Company/Closing Attorney

Locating title companies is simple; finding a *good* one is a little more challenging. Most title groups deal with traditional transactions every day and never really step outside of that realm of real estate. They may rarely, if ever, deal with investors or the types of transactions you will be focusing on while getting your investment business up and running. I say this as a warning. Don't get frustrated and give up because the first 10 title companies you call turn you down or are confused about what you are looking to do. It's 100% not your fault; the fault really lies with their lack of education and training. We can't worry about what others don't understand. This goes for attorneys, too! You will be amazed how many attorneys and real estate professionals have never dealt with a wholesale transaction.

There is a multitude of ways to find a great title company. The single best way is through referral from another investor. You may be thinking, *I don't know any investors at this point*, and that's perfectly fine. This is expected, and I will explain other ways to find solid team members, but just know there is no better way to find a great team member or title group than word of mouth. Experienced investors are always looking to share the great experiences they have had with companies because they have had to wade through the bad to get to the good. So, once you begin marketing and networking, don't hesitate to ask for title company and closing attorney referrals.

If you don't happen to know anyone already investing and need another way to locate a title group to close your transactions, you can do the next best thing and ask "Google." Simply enter your current location along with the phrase "real estate title group" or "real estate attorney" in the search box.

Example: Northeast Ohio Real Estate Title Group

This quick search will pull up hundreds of title companies in many cases, and you will want to begin to build a list of contact numbers and names to call. Shortly, I will discuss word-for-word what to say to find a company that will work best for you. But for now just begin to gather a list of title companies and contact information because it will take more than one call. It took me no less than 20 calls when I was initially looking for a title group. You can further refine your search by reading the reviews and comments on each company. If you find a group that has good reviews or even a testimonial from an investor, you might start there. Below is an example of a review and testimonial for the title company I use:

★★★★★ in the last week - Edit
I have had no better experience with a title group than Fireland Title. I have had the pleasure of closing investment deals as well as my personal home with them and there has been nothing but quality experiences. The team is friendly and VERY responsive to any questions that you may have. I don't have have title work done anywhere else. Quick Story about how personal they are and the experience they create. I recently had my first child. We had a closing just a few weeks ago and the agent put out my closing docs and he had "closing Docs" out for my son as well. the closing documents were a coloring book and crayons... Tell me where else you can get service and attention like that? If you are looking for a title group... look no further.

If you find a review similar to this for a title company you find, call them! Note that the above review mentions personal connection and investment deals. This is gold! You won't always be able to find great reviews, though. Unfortunately, many people only leave reviews if they have had a poor experience and don't bother to leave one when they have a great experience.

The third and final way to find a great title company is to use the yellow pages in the phone book. I can hear you groan as you read this, but, yes, phone books are still a real thing and a great way to find businesses. This might be the most inefficient way to find a title group, but if you don't have access to the internet, this can be a solid option.

No matter how you find the title company or attorney that you will be using, you will need to know what to say and what to ask so that you can determine if they will be a good fit for your business. So, let's go over that next!

GREAT QUESTION: AM I FOLLOWING THE STEPS OF THE SUCCESSFUL TO BUILD MY OWN SUCCESS, OR AM I MODIFYING THE PROCESS FOR SOME REASON?

Title Company/Attorney Script

I am providing you a script to follow to help you locate the perfect title group for your business. It will guide you through the phone call so that you will know exactly what to expect as the call progresses. As I mentioned before, it will probably take an afternoon of calling companies to find one that is a good fit for you. Remember, don't get discouraged. Simply move on to the next title company and begin the conversation again until you nail one down that you will be excited to work with. Below each section of the script is a short description of what to expect so that when you start this process on your own, you will know you are on the right track. Happy hunting!

Script 1

Questions you should be asking in this exact order:

Title Company Gate Keeper: Hi, thank you for calling "X" Title Company. How can I help you?

You: Hi! May I speak with a closing agent?

Title Company Gate Keeper: Absolutely. I will get you over to an agent right away. Can I ask what this is about? Do you have a question about a deal?

You: Yes, I do. I need to ask a couple of specific questions about my current deal and upcoming transactions.

Title Company Gate Keeper: Ok. I will transfer you over. Hang on one second.

Title Company Closing Agent: (Always ask to speak to the person you will be dealing with or who makes the decisions.) Hi. This is "Agent X." I hear you have a few questions about a closing. Do you have the deal here with us already?

You: I do not. Not yet. I have a couple of questions about the types of closings that your company handles. I am calling to see if you can complete double closing transactions or assignments of contract.

Title Company Closing Agent: What is a double closing?

You: For example, I have a property under contract to purchase for $50,000, but I want to sell it before I close on it because I already have a buyer committed to buying it from me for $65,000. Can we come to closing together so we can close "back-to back," or simultaneously, so that the property goes from the seller, to me, to the buyer immediately? I plan on bringing the funds for closing on the first transaction, but I want to make sure that we can close the second portion of the deal with the final buyer the same day, or within 24 hours.

Title Company Closing Agent: I have never heard of that...

You: What about an assignment of contract?

Title Company Closing Agent: I think that's illegal. Are you a licensed agent?

You: No, I am not. I am just selling the contract, though, not collecting a commission.

Title Company Closing Agent: I will need to look into it. I will call you back.

You: Thank you for keeping me in mind.

END SCRIPT 1

This is more than likely how the first handful of calls you make will go. You will get a lot of confused reactions, along with doubt and skepticism. Luckily, you will be prepared for this through this guide, so you will know what is right and what is wrong. After a conversation like this, you simply move on to the next company or attorney on your list. As mentioned before, not every title group deals with investors, so you are a bit of an anomaly to them at times.

SCRIPT 2

Title Company Gate Keeper: Hi. Thank you for calling "X" Title Company. How can I help you?

You: Hi! May I speak with a closing agent?

Title Company Gate Keeper: Absolutely. I will transfer you to an agent right away. Can I ask what this is about? Do you have a question about a deal?

You: Yes, I do. I need to ask a couple of specific questions about my current deal and upcoming transactions.

Title Company Gate Keeper: Ok. I will transfer you right over. Hang on one second.

Title Company Closing Agent: (Always ask to speak to the person you will be dealing with or who makes the decisions.) Hi. This is "Agent X." I hear you have a few questions about a closing. Do you have the deal here with us already?

You: I do not. Not yet. I have a couple of questions about the types of closings that your company handles. I am calling to see if you can complete double closing transactions or assignments of contract.

Title Company Closing Agent: When you say "double closing," do you mean a simultaneous closing or A-B-C Transaction?

You: YES! That's exactly what I am looking to do. For example, if I have a property under contract for $50k, I want to be able either to sell my contract for a fee or complete a double

9

closing so that the property goes from the seller to me to the end buyer in a few moments, with the transactions filed back to back.

Title Company Closing Agent: Yes, we can do that. We do this for investors all over the area.

You: That's fantastic! Can you handle assignments also?

Title Company Closing Agent: You want to sell your contract for a fee? Do you have an assignment sheet on which everyone has signed off on each detail of the transaction?

You: Yes. Yes, I do.

Title Company Closing Agent: Yes, we can handle that, too.

You: Awesome! That's great news. I plan on doing a lot of business through your company. How long does it typically take you to close a deal?

Title Company Closing Agent: It really depends on the situation and how clean the title work comes back, but we will get it done as fast and as efficiently as we can.

You: Perfect! Many times we will need to close quickly, and it sounds like that's a possibility.

I appreciate your time. I have only one last question. Can I have a copy of your "For Sale By Owner" package? I would like to use your purchase contract if you have a copy I could borrow.

Title Company Closing Agent: Of course. I will send it to you now.

You: Thanks so much for your time. I will be in touch shortly.

END SCRIPT 2

As you can tell, in this script you found yourself a title company. CONGRATULATIONS! You just completed Step 1. Find a title company that can complete the deals you need, and you can start building relationships with them to work together weekly. This will become an important asset. This title company and the relationships you have with the people within the company will become some of the most important you have in this business. You are building a team around you, and this part of the team gets your deals done.

GREAT QUESTION: AM I LOOKING TO PROVIDE VALUE BACK TO THE PEOPLE WHO ARE GOING TO BE PROVIDING VALUE TO ME?

Wrapping up Title Company/Attorney

The search for a good, solid title company that you will want to do multiple deals with can feel lonely at times, but shouldn't be all that stressful overall. Keep it simple. Ask the few specific questions provided in the scripts in the section above, and you will be on your way to building a relationship with a great closing agent in no time. Following the scripts above will enable you to find someone trustworthy and experienced. Following the scripts line-by-line as I have suggested might come off as a bit robotic at first, but it will become natural after only a couple calls.

Last, but not least: note that when you find a title group that you are able to work with, you should request their company's "For Sale By Owner" package. This package contains the title group's own purchase agreement, so the title company team will be very well versed in it and understand all of the details of it. This will enable them to deal with any questions they may have about the contract and can help speed up the closing process since they are intimately familiar with their company's purchase agreement, which will not be the case if you use a contract sourced from another company. Next up: Networking with Buyers!

GREAT QUESTION: AM I KEEPING THINGS SIMPLE, OR AM I OVERCOMPLICATING THINGS OUT OF FEAR?

Step Two

Networking With Buyers

That's right. You read that correctly. Step two, the next step you need to take after locating a title company, is to begin networking with buyers. This is where most people go wrong. Many new investors want to begin finding properties next, but that puts them at risk because they then have to do a lot of guessing. Let me explain what I mean.

The goal in wholesaling is to connect a buyer to a seller. You are trying to solve problems for sellers by helping them out of stressful situations involving property. You cannot sell your contracts or close on properties with sellers without having buyers. If you place a property under contract that needs sold in less than two weeks because it is going to the auction block due to foreclosure, and you promise the seller you will stop the foreclosure and then fail to find a buyer in time, you become part of the problem. You let the seller down and failed to perform on your word. This is bad from every standpoint. This will kill your reputation and, honestly, it should. When you gamble with other people's emotions and properties, you are playing with fire. You and your seller will both be burned at some point. This is not a sustainable business model.

Use this mantra in running your business: "I am looking for properties for buyers, not looking for buyers for properties." What this means is that you are not putting properties under contract and locking them up until you find someone who wants to buy it. This is unethical and flat out wrong. Anyone who teaches this or practices this type of real estate investing is giving investors a bad name, and you should steer clear of this type of person. These types are only concerned with themselves. Locating buyers for properties before ever putting a property under contract will ensure that you will sell your contracts and perform every time you have a purchase agreement with a seller. This will improve your confidence and build a positive reputation for yourself, which will, in turn, bring you more business and improve the lives of everyone around you.

Locating good, quality buyers before looking for sellers will also help refine your search for properties and eliminate any guesswork in doing so. If you have no buyers, then what are you looking for? What kind of property will the buyers you eventually line up want? What areas should you be hunting in? What kind of condition should the property be in before you put your signature on the dotted line? Will your buyers want to hold the property as a rental, or will they want to flip the property to a retail buyer? What are your buyer's goals? What will their time frame for closing be if the seller needs to sell fast? If the seller needs cash as soon as possible, will your buyer be able to come in and close quickly with a cash transaction? If the property is in bad condition, will your buyer have a budget to fix the property? Will your buyer have any relationships with laborers so that the work that needs done isn't as expensive? What is expensive to you? What will your buyer define as expensive?

You see how the guessing game begins to snowball out of control? If you start your journey in wholesaling real estate by just searching for distressed homeowners, you are in for a rude awakening. You will struggle to get properties under contract at the right price, and you will struggle to sell properties to buyers in the time allotted. You will end up frustrated and annoyed with your ineffective business model.

Now that we understand why we don't skimp on our buyer relationships, let's discuss the upsides to having a buyer in place before ever signing a contract with a seller. To do so, let's address a few common questions about our buyers.

1. Q. Should I have a lot of buyers lined up before I find properties?
   a. You need only a couple of legitimate relationships with solid buyers to begin finding properties for them, being confident that they will perform as discussed.
2. Q. Do my buyers need the cash up front to close quickly?
   a. The common response to this question is, "Yes. The buyer needs to be in a cash-in-hand position to work with you." In reality, this is FALSE. They don't need to be a cash buyer to be a great partner. You can assign contracts to any type of buyer. We will discuss this in extreme detail later in the book
3. Q. If my buyer backs out for some reason, am I stuck with the property?
   a. The whole point of this section is to ensure that you're picking confident and capable buyers, but this does occasionally happen. However, should this happen, you will not be stuck with the property because you will have legal contingencies (outs) in place to protect you. I will address this in detail in the contracts

portion of the Signing Purchase Agreements with Sellers section.

4. Q. My buyer needs to get a loan for the property I have under contract. Is this possible?
   a. Yes. The property will need to stand up to the underwriting process of the loan, but the short answer is "yes."
5. Q. My buyer wants a 30-day due diligence period to inspect the property.
   a. That's great! Communicate this to the seller and insert a specific due diligence period in the original contract with the seller.
6. Q. Is it possible to switch buyers after signing with them if I get a higher offer elsewhere?
   a. No, you must sell to the first buyer you signed with. This is the ethical and right thing to do. In the future remember this happened and try reworking your numbers or contacting other buyers before signing a contract with the first offer you get.
7. Q. My buyer wants to negotiate terms for the property and pay monthly to purchase the property. Is this possible?
   a. Yes! You can negotiate so that the buyer can make payments to the seller for a property.

These are just a few questions that will be addressed more fully in this section about our buyers and future purchasing partners. As you gain experience and speak with more people, you will get a feel for what type of buyer each one is and how to best utilize them in your business.

At this point I like to remind people the massive value that you are bringing to the buyer. Many buyers struggle to locate properties at a discount. You will be an expert in this field and well known for bringing great deals to investors. This is what you are being paid to do. You bring value to the marketplace by locating and solving problems. The more you practice this the better you will get at locating problems and plugging in different types of buyers to help solve these issues. As a result, you will be paid handsomely. Be proud; you have earned it!

GREAT QUESTION: AM I LOCATING PROPERTIES FOR BUYERS, OR AM I HUNTING FOR BUYERS IN A PANIC AFTER LOCKING UP A PROPERTY UNDER CONTRACT OUT OF ORDER?

Where to Find Buyers

Buyers are everywhere! That's the good news. No, that's the great news! I am going to teach you how to locate these people and get them excited about working alongside you. Bringing on a great team member is all about your ability to bring value to their life and their business. If you are out working hard for them, you better believe they will be out in the field working hard for you. This is what creates a great relationship and the start of an empire. Below are specific steps to take for locating fellow investors and buying partners.

1. Local Networking and Meetups: Never underestimate the power of local networking. What do I mean when I say local networking? I am focusing on structured organization, such as REIA (Real Estate Investors Association), meetings and local real estate investment groups. These groups are extremely common and are packed with quality investors, both new and experienced. Attending these

events will allow you to meet with multiple groups of investors on a weekly or monthly basis.

    a. There are a couple of good resources to use to locate these groups. The best is typically www.meetup.com. This website is designed for organizing local meetups for all different types of activities and topics far and wide. Real estate is just one of the many you will find on here. I recommend you type in your local zip code so that you can find the closest meetings and begin going to them and letting people know what you are looking to do. The more people you can tell about what you are doing the better! Also, don't be scared to use the word "wholesale" or "wholesaler" at these meetings. The investors understand what you are looking to do, and you will have buyers flock to you during these meetings to get you to help locate opportunities for them.

    b. Another great source for finding local groups is www.EventBrite.com. This site is similar to MeetUp.com and will allow you to locate local groups meeting for real estate training and investment. Both of these sites are great options. You can search for your local zip code, or you can search key words, such as "real estate" or "investing," to nail down the meetings you should be attending. These meetings are typically free, although some will occasionally cost a couple dollars to cover the expenses associated with the meeting venue. Either way, you should be able to attend for free for a short period of time before committing anything. What's great about these local meetups is that they commonly have mass emailing lists set up that you can sign up to get. This contacts

list will provide you with 100-plus email addresses of people buying in the area. Talk about an instant "buyers list"!
2. Online Ads: Free online ads are an often overlooked asset in the real estate community.

   a. The most common and effective tool in my opinion is www.Craigslist.Org. Most people have heard of Craigslist. If you haven't, it is a site that is set up so that you can offer services, post items for sale, and post ads stating that you are in search of certain talents or objects for free. In this case we will be posting ads in specified sections stating that we are looking for buying partners. I will give you a full rundown on where, when, how often, and exactly what to post later on in this section.

   b. The next best place to be posting for buyers and partners will be on all of your social media accounts. I love Facebook! Facebook is so overwhelmingly popular these days that you can post a simple status that can become a networking gold mine for you. Simply post that you are involved in real estate and are looking for other people to network with who are also involved in real estate. Almost immediately, you will have, say, 30 people replying to you, tagging people they know in real estate, and others who come forward and explain what they do within the real estate industry. Again, I will give you a specific guide on what, where, and how often to post on your Facebook account.

   c. Did you know you can easily locate buyers and investors in your area on Instagram? Instagram is less popular than Facebook, but there is a hidden gem within Instagram. If you search your local area for specific hashtags, such as #Flipping_____, inserting your market name on the blank line, you will find people posting pictures of their projects in your area. These are obviously real buyers and investors because they are posting pictures of their progress day to day. You can send these people messages and ask what kind of property and deals they like so that you can start finding them property. You can play with this and try all sorts of different real estate oriented hashtags, such as #Flipping, #Fixing, #FixNFlip, #Renting, #Leasing, #BuyingHouses, #SellingHouses, #Wholesaling, etc. This strategy may not bring you a large number of buyers, but the couple that it can bring could be the opportunity you are looking for. Don't forget to insert the market or location you are interested in so that you aren't contacting people in the wrong markets.

3. A couple of my personal favorites are Property Management Companies and Title Groups. You can do a quick online search for property management companies in your area, and you can also speak with the title groups in your market. The conversation will have to be structured slightly different from normal because these companies will be protecting the identity and information of their investors and buyers, but you can certainly call them and offer your services and allow them to pass on your contact information to anyone looking to buy more real estate. You would be amazed how well this works and how many calls you will get directly using this word-of-mouth technique.

4. ==Insurance Agents== are great contacts for finding investors and property owners. This conversation will be similar to those you have with the property management and title companies in that you will more than likely need to leave your contact information with them and trust them to pass it on to their contacts. Have faith in this strategy! At the time of writing this book one of my absolute best partners has come from an insurance agent referral. The referral game is strong!

5. ==Real Estate Agents== should always be on your list of contacts for ==leveraging multiple networks at once==. When you are looking for a specific buyer or criteria, many times realtors will have someone who can help or point you in the right direction. The nice part about realtors is that there are so many of them. Try to speak with as many agents as possible and let them know what you are doing so that you continue to get your name out as much as possible. Many times when a licensed agent has an investing buyer, they will be looking for off-market properties, and guess who will be supplying those? You guessed it! You! You should be in the phone contact list of every agent in the area.

6. Word of Mouth is the most powerful tool on the planet. Telling absolutely everyone what you do and asking a great question like, "Do you know anyone looking for a great real estate deal?" will go a long way. This will bring you opportunities from every direction and market.

7. Flyers and Business Cards are a tried and true option for getting your name out into the world and finding great

buying partners. Where do you put them? Everywhere! The beauty of cards and flyers is that they are either free or super cheap, assuming you can print your own. You can place these under the windshield wipers of cars and trucks at stores like Home Depot and Lowe's, where people are buying items for houses. If you hit the lots very early in the morning, you can almost assure yourself of some calls from contractors, whose vehicles you hit with a piece of marketing. Your flyer can be super simple as well; it doesn't have to be anything overcomplicated. It can say something as simple as, **"Todd Buys and Sells Houses at Discount Call Or Text Todd at (Phone number) if you are interested in buying more houses!"** See how simple that is? That is quick and easy to read and will surely bring calls your way.

8. Bandit Signs are the signs you see stapled to telephone poles and in the grassy areas near busy intersections that state, "We Buy Houses!" You know why you see them out there? They work! This is a more costly form of marketing for buyers, but it can be a great way to find people looking to work with others. To give you an idea of how well it works, I call every single bandit sign I see to find out if they have a deal for me. Other investors do the same. Again, much like the flyer, the sign can be very simple and just state that you buy and sell houses at a discount and are looking for partners. You can find bandit signs for sale on a number of online sites. Simply search "real estate bandit sign," and you will have a handful of choices from which to choose.

9. The MLS (Multiple Listing Service) can be a wonderful tool for specific search results. The MLS is the software system used by the marketplace that every realtor has access to that lists every house and property that is listed for sale

and has been sold and recorded. You can have a realtor do a search for the most recent transactions in a specific area that were cash transactions. A bulk of cash transactions can be a good sign of investors. This search will also occasionally provide contact information for those buyers, which will enable you to reach out and introduce yourself.

10. The most expensive way of marketing toward buyers is through Direct Mailing. If you have no budget for marketing at this time, it's okay; you can find plenty of buyers without mailing any marketing material to them. This is just another option to keep in mind once you begin to scale your business and want to expand your reach even further. You can obtain the tax mailing address of anyone who has completed a cash transaction and mail your information to them, asking if they are looking to purchase more property. This is not only expensive, but it can be less efficient than the other forms of marketing yourself. To locate the tax mailing address go to the county fiscal office real estate search website and type in the addresses of the properties that were purchased via cash from the MLS search mentioned in Method 9 above. This will pull up detailed information on the property. To attempt to reach the person who bought the property, mail your information to the tax mailing address you find listed. Don't mail it to the physical address that the MLS search pulled up because you will likely be mailing to the renter in place. You want to make sure you are contacting the absentee owner of the property. If the tax mailing address is the same as the physical property, it is likely that it is not an investor deal, so sort those out and avoid mailing to those properties and save your time and money. The information in the letter you mail can be identical to the information you provide

on your flyer and bandit signs. Simply introduce yourself and state that you buy and sell property at a discount. If they are interested in more, they will call you.

11. It is always important to stand out from the crowd and try new tactics for advertising yourself. A favorite one that I have seen used is the placement of stickers on gas pumps stating that they buy houses. They have stickers printed up, and they put them on the "87" gas pump button, so A LOT of people see it. I think that's fantastic. I have personally left my business card at every station at hair salons and barbershops. Barbers see and meet everyone! If you are able to leave your card at everyone's station, you are very likely to run into an investor getting a quick cut. These are just a couple more quick examples of ways to get your name out there and to think BIG and think creatively!

GREAT QUESTION: AM I ADVERTISING MYSELF EVERYWHERE THAT I CAN SO THAT I CAN CAPITALIZE ON AS MUCH OPPORTUNITY AS POSSIBLE?

What to Say and What Questions to Ask

Now that we have an entire playbook of ways to locate buyers, what do we say to ensure we are locating and working with great partners? I will cover what to look for and what questions to be sure to ask so that you can gauge who is serious and who might be just kicking tires. It's important to note that nothing beats experience when it comes to talking to potential partners, so don't be scared to just talk to as many people as possible. Experienced investors are always looking to help and work with new and upcoming partners. Real estate is the most unique business in the world, in my opinion. I have found very little haste and hate inside this game. I feel everyone is looking out for each other for the most part. It is amazing to see how everyone helps when everyone has similar goals and a similar mindset.

I will provide different types of marketing examples as well. I will cover specific scripts and exact examples that I myself post every day, so make sure to pay close attention and try to model what I put out to the world as closely as possible. The ads that I place and the structure of my ads have been tested over and over, and I am sharing my best ones with you today in this book. To best cover each scenario I will roleplay multiple types of interactions, including both local meets and phone conversations. I will also present a great way to explain what it is that you do in real estate when someone puts you on the spot so that it piques interest and sparks further conversation.

First, let's cover the dialogue that follows when a potential buying partner who has gotten one of your marketing pieces calls you. The conversation will be similar no matter how they learned of you. The most important thing to remember is that when someone calls you, you should be sparking conversation and asking great questions so that you can listen to the answers and understand how you can help that person in the best way possible. A point I like to stress for new and experienced investors alike is that you are building a reputation and a brand. Make sure you stand out, even when they aren't able to reach you on the first call. This means you should make sure your voicemail recording is set up so that your message exhibits excitement and doesn't just say, "Leave your message after the beep." Let the potential caller know you mean business by recording something like, "Hey, thanks for calling! You have reached Todd. If this is about a house, please leave a detailed message regarding how I can help, and I will get back to you before the end of the day!" See how that captures the caller's attention better than just, "Leave a message after the beep?" This will help with call retention, which can put extra opportunity on your desk and extra loot in your pocket!

When the first call comes in, you will be terrified. So expect that. I have a mental hack to conquer this immediately, though. Read this carefully and understand it fully, and you will never be nervous on the phone again. The conscious human mind can only think and worry about one thing at a time. We aren't multitaskers. If you find your phone ringing, or you're nervous about returning a phone call, remember this fact: ==if you are worrying about yourself, you are not doing your job and trying to help others solve problems.== If you flip your mindset and worry about the other person, the person who is calling, and realize that they have a potential problem and are in pain, you can't worry about yourself anymore. You can't be nervous anymore. It's physically impossible. Try this! I promise it works. You will never be nervous on the phone again after you practice this tactic. If you find yourself nervous or scared at any point during this process, you are worrying about yourself and not the other person. Flip it!

Now that we understand how to handle our emotions so that we can actually pick up the phone, we can start our conversation. The main focus is to be polite and open-minded and ask great questions to get the potential buyer talking about his goals and what his criteria might be so that you know exactly what type of property to hunt for. This is also a great time to set expectations.

Don't lead someone to believe that you have property ready for them when you don't. Unfortunately, it isn't uncommon for people to post fake Craigslist ads or online ads stating that they have this great deal ready for the first person to come up with the cash, and then they pull the bait and switch when the phone rings and tell the investor that the deal has already been sold. This type of ad has been called many different names, but "ghost ad" seems to be the most prominent way of describing these fake ads. This tactic is unethical and can hurt your business. This puts a bad taste in the mouth of the potential buyer and can sabotage your business before you even get started, so don't go down this route when marketing for partners. Remember the name of the game is honest, ethical, and transparent.

Now that we have calls coming in, let's look at how a conversation could occur from start to finish.

Begin Buyer Script

You: Hello, this is "Todd."

Buyer: Hey, is this Todd from the online ads that say you have discounted houses for sale?

You: Hey! Yes it is. How are you doing today? What's your name?

Buyer: Hey, I'm Brandon. I was calling to see if you had anything to sell right now and what kind of houses you find. I'm an investor, and I'm always looking for more houses.

You: That's great! I would love to help you reach any goals that you have. How many houses are you looking to buy this year?

Buyer: I will buy as many as I can get my hands on, honestly. It's just a matter of finding the right deals.

You: I hear that! That's what I do. I commonly find properties at deep discounts and sell them to other investors or hold onto them myself.

Buyer: That's perfect. How do you find them?

You: I market–A LOT. I will target any area that you want, so I can help you reach your goals. Where do you like to buy? What zip codes specifically?

Buyer: I like to buy in 44314, 44306, and 44312, but I will buy anywhere if the numbers work.

You: I can definitely help with that. What kind of price range do you prefer?

Buyer: I like to be in the 100-150 range so that I can sell closer to 200-225.

You: Okay, perfect. Those are definitely doable in those areas. If I were to bring you multiple deals in a month, would you be able to handle more than one project?

Buyer: YES (Or no... doesn't matter)

You: Okay, great. We can work together on that. How do you typically like to pay for your properties?

Buyer: Depends what I have going on, honestly. I try to use cash, but sometimes grab funding elsewhere.

You: Beautiful! Last couple questions for you, real quick. Do you like just to flip? Or do you buy and hold also for wealth creation and passive income?

Buyer: I buy and hold also. (If they just flip, that's fine, too. This question is designed to gauge if you should send them every property you find or only flips/rentals.)

You: Nice! I am building a portfolio myself. How many do you own, if you don't mind my asking?

Buyer: Seven. (Any number greater than one, and you send them every deal that you find.)

You: Killer! Last two questions, and I'll let you go, my friend. What did your last few deals look like, and have you ever considered what your DREAM deal would look like? I personally have always wanted to own an apartment building.

Buyer: My last few deals were in those few zip codes I listed, and I picked them up at auction. I feel like I paid a little too much, but overall they worked out. We flipped them all for a profit.

Buyer: Man..ummm.. dream deal, that's a good question. I'd love to flip a million dollar home. (THIS MEANS THE MINDSET AND CAPITAL ARE AVAILABLE TO DO IT), and an apartment building would be great! (This indicates he or she is open to long-term, passive income.)

You: Well, I will certainly keep that in mind! I will let you go now. Thanks so much for reaching out. I'm looking forward to working together. I will have marketing going out, and anything that fits your criteria I will send your way first! Do you prefer me to call, text, or email?

Buyer: Any and all work. My email is Buyersemailexample@Gmail.com. Nice talking to you!

You: Hi, Sarah. My name is Todd. I buy and sell property at a discount. Have you ever thought of investing in real estate?

Buyer: No, I haven't.

You: Hmm...why?

End Script Two

As you can see, your answer is exactly the same! No matter how they answer, you simply ask them, "Why?" This is an open door for you to learn what is on their mind and what their opinion is of real estate and investing. This conversation can lead to great relationships or just a simple short talk. Either way, you are letting everyone know what you do in a simple precise format that will get you deals. If the person states, "Yes," they have thought of investing in real estate before, and the conversation continues, you can begin to ask them the questions listed below to get a perfect idea of their experience level and how you can help:

30 Great Questions To Ask Potential Buying Partners:

1. Where do you like to buy?
2. What type of property are you looking to purchase? Single family? Multi-family?
3. What did your last five deals look like?
4. Do you stick to a certain criteria?
5. Do you prefer holding for rental income, or flipping? Do you do both?

6. How do you like to pay for your investments? With cash, or do you use financing?
7. Can you close quickly? What time frame works best for you?
8. Do you like to walk each property, or do you buy sight unseen?
9. Have you ever bought from a wholesaler before?
10. What are your goals this year?
11. How many properties do you own, if you don't mind my asking?
12. Do you manage your own properties?
13. What does your dream deal look like? Do you know what it is?
14. Do you have the ability to take on multiple projects at once?
15. Do you typically make the decisions, or do you use partners as well?
16. How can I best help you reach your goals?
17. I commonly look to assign contracts. Is that okay with you?
18. Do you have a specific title group that you prefer to use?
19. Do you have a specific contract that you prefer to use?
20. Do you have any other investors that you think I should meet and help as well?
21. Do you have any current deals on the table right now?
22. What price range do you like to be in when purchasing?

23. Do you prefer I contact you via email, text, or phone call?
24. I work with investors all over the area. Would you like to connect with more people?
25. What is the maximum number of properties you could handle in a month?
26. Do you plan on investing forever?
27. How did you get started?
28. Do you invest full time?
29. Why real estate?
30. Do you enjoy larger projects, or would you rather have properties that need minimal work?

The goal is to build rapport with buyers and figure out what will best help them. Asking great questions is the only way to find out what they really need in their business. You obviously won't ask all of these questions during the first phone call or meeting, but over a handful of conversations you will learn what this buyer's potential problem is and how you can help solve it. You will become a valuable asset to his or her team, and you will build a reputation for finding and closing great deals.

All of the questions above unlock important information about your potential partner. They gauge interest and measure capability. Each question brings a specific value to your relationship. Each question will help you take one step closer to your first wholesale transaction in real estate. All you have to do now is to be consistent in your networking and talk to as many people as possible so that you can build great relationships with a few different buyers across your market and go to work finding them properties!

Now that we know how to handle incoming calls and talk with fellow investors, it's time to start talking with potential sellers.

GREAT QUESTION: AM I WORRYING ABOUT MYSELF, OR AM I WORRYING ABOUT THE CALLER'S POTENTIAL PAIN?

---

fallen behind in paying the property taxes and now no longer has the ability to cover the bill and needs to sell.

==Liquidation:== Many people would rather not pass down property and the responsibility thereof after passing away. As a result, sellers will liquidate their assets when they get older, or when they are comfortable with no longer owning.

==Down Markets:== When a market hits a recession, people who are either overleveraged or have lost their jobs need solutions to bring in money. It is not uncommon for people to sell their homes in downturns. You can be of help even if the property is underwater (worth less than what is owed).

Moving to New Home: When moving into a new property, sellers need to sell their old property to help pay for their new home.

Out-of-State Seller: There are a multitude of reasons for why family members or friends end up with property hundreds of miles from where they live. In this situation, it is best for them to sell and relieve themselves of the responsibility of owning another home they will never see.

Seller Wants To Reinvest Sale Funds Into New Deal: There are times when a new investment opportunity has presented itself to a seller, and to take it, he needs to sell a property.

==Poor Lending Terms:== This means that whoever or however they secured funds to pay for the house is no longer working for them. This could mean that the payment is higher than the rental income they can receive or that they can no longer make the mortgage (loan) payments.

House Expenses: The house is in poor or worsening condition, and the seller can't keep up with the maintenance expenses.

Deferred Maintenance: Similar to the seller's not being able to pay for updates or maintenance, but in this scenario the property is in such poor condition that the seller doesn't want to take on the daunting task of fixing everything. The work may even cost more than what the house is worth in certain markets.

Health Code Violations: Sellers are required to update a home or clean up a property because its living conditions have been determined to be below code. An example of this is hoarder houses. (I have experience with hoarder houses; they are a handful!)

Emotional Reasons: There is no shortage of emotional turning points in which someone needs to sell or liquidate a property.

Lessen Responsibility: Some people are motivated to sell so they can be renters again. Renting is far less time consuming and holds less responsibility, so the seller can focus on other aspects of life.

Downsizing: Parents sell their homes after the kids move out because they no longer need the extra room. It is common for older generations to want to move into ranch-style homes (single floor) to avoid staircases.

The above examples represent a SMALL sample size of possible reasons to sell a property. Trust me when I say every day you will discover new reasons for why people need to sell and why you need to help them accomplish just that. With all of these reasons to sell, how can we possibly have a solution for all of them? One word: Practice! In the beginning, you may be overwhelmed or confused about how to pinpoint the problem or how to solve it. This is totally natural and expected. You can't learn and look good at the same time, remember?

GREAT QUESTION: WHY DO YOU WANT TO SELL?

Locating Problems to Solve

Now that we are aware of just a small fraction of the possible problems sellers face, we need to practice locating these problems. Better yet, we need to learn how to discover these problems by asking great questions and consistently marketing ourselves as problem solvers.

Our focus in the beginning is to build a large network so that we have potential sellers approach us and ask us to be their personal problem solver. To do this, we will be putting our name out into the world everywhere we go. When the leads begin to funnel into us, we will begin the process of uncovering the real problem at hand. Not everything is what it seems. To learn the source of a seller's pain, we need to ask great questions, build rapport, and feel genuine empathy. In doing so, we lower the walls surrounding the seller's ego, and then–and only then–we can solve his or her problem. People sell to people they like and trust. You need to be more likeable than the next guy. You do this by actually caring about the situation at hand and asking questions about the seller. The next section is on building rapport.

GREAT QUESTION: HOW WOULD I FEEL IF I WERE IN THIS SELLER'S SITUATION?

Rapport Building

Building rapport is a learned skill. Whether you are an introvert or extremely outgoing and talkative doesn't matter much. Regardless, you will be starting at the base problem and working your way up. The first time you meet a seller at a property you will feel out of place. You will feel strange. You may actually feel like a bit of a fraud at first because in many cases people just starting out don't have the money or network to purchase the property. Luckily, you are following this process step by step and know in the back of your mind that even if you don't have the funds to purchase the properties, your partners do. That thought should give you the confidence that you belong there. Remember the value you are bringing to this distressed situation. You are meant to be there. So, don't worry too much and focus on the two most important things you should be doing:

1. Ask great questions.
2. Listen.

Sounds simple enough, right? However, you would be amazed how much we tend to get chatty and/or not listen intently when we are in an uncomfortable situation. Don't be surprised if the first time you leave a property walkthrough with a seller, you don't remember anything that he or she said. This will improve quickly over time. Again, expect this, and don't be ashamed if it happens to you.

Asking questions is the most proven approach for building rapport. Why is that? It's because people love to talk about themselves. When you truly listen to the answers and the sellers' story, they will respect you and put you on a higher pedestal. Think back to a time when someone wouldn't shut up about themselves and their life. How did you feel about that individual? Now think about someone who is a great listener and who you can count on to call if you need to talk to someone. How do you feel about that person? Make sure you fall into the latter category. Be the powerful listener. Below are some great questions to ask a seller:

GREAT QUESTIONS TO ASK

How long have you owned the home?

How long did you live here?

Are there any really cool stories that you can tell me about the property?

Who first bought the home?

What are your goals with the house?

Have you ever thought about fixing the property up yourself?

How can I best serve you?

Have you ever dealt with a buyer before?

Have you ever sold a home before?

Do you understand how the home buying and selling process works?

Where would you like to move?

What would you like to see happen to the home?

How quickly would you like to close?

How would you like to be paid?

Are there any structural issues with the property?

Are there any major issues that I should address first?

How old is the house?

Did you know the previous owners?

Would you like to come back and see the house when it is finished?

Why do you want to sell?

The final question in this batch is the most powerful question you can ask a seller. You must never forget to ask why. When you ask why they want to sell, shut up and listen! People with a real problem will tell you all about it, given the opportunity. If you listen carefully, you will then be able to unearth the true problem at hand and help them solve it. You will become their knight in shining armor. Uncovering motivation is an art form. You need to be ethically strong to be doing this, as well. If someone were to do this simply to manipulate someone, shame on that person. This is meant to be a tool for helping, not conquering.

The answers to the above questions will range from typical to over-the-top crazy. No matter how they answer them, it is more important that you are listening closely and discovering the true pain at hand. You should be listening 80% of the time, at a minimum.

GREAT QUESTION: WHY DO YOU WANT TO SELL?

Marketing to Problems

In order to listen and build rapport, we need people to talk to us. In this section we are going to discuss marketing tactics to expand our ability to reach more people more effectively. To design a great deal, we need to investigate every possible opportunity. There are endless ways to market yourself and your brand. Given the myriad of methods to market yourself, I want to ensure that you are doing it effectively and not just mindlessly marketing without any direction.

With so many ways to market ourselves, how do we choose which route to take? How do we choose which vehicle to use to leverage ourselves as much as possible at the best price and in the shortest amount of time? One deciding factor is your budget. If you are like I was, I didn't have anything left for a marketing budget after getting my real estate license and paying all of the miscellaneous fees that go along with it. So I will first discuss free and extremely affordable avenues that you can use initially and discuss more expensive strategies later on in this book. You will recognize many of these tactics because they are very similar to the ones used to find buyers and investing partners. We will change the wording of our advertisements and the locations we target, but, basically, all the marketing techniques discussed earlier in this book work. You just need to retarget them accordingly.

1. **Online Ads – Craigslist:** Use Craigslist.Org to get your ads out for free every day. The best part about Craigslist is that it is so well known that the number of daily visitors to this website is absurd. You will not only be able to search through the "for sale" section to find sellers with property that matches the criteria of your buyers, but you will also be able to post your own advertisements multiple times per day. Craigslist has a timeline on it that you can scroll through. It functions very much like any social media site. The newest postings and listings are at the top, and the farther you scroll down, the older the ads are. This is an advantage for us! This is advantageous for us because we are going to own that entire timeline. You should be posting your "Todd Buys Houses/We Buy Houses" logo five to ten times per day–five in the morning, five at night. After a few weeks of doing this, you will solidify a spot everywhere on the immediate timeline that someone will scroll through while looking for whatever it is they are searching.

    You want to be posting each ad in different sections as well. For example, post five ads in the morning in the following sections: Real Estate Services, Real Estate For Sale, Real Estate Wanted, Wanted by Owner, General Community. When posting in these different sections, you will want to be posting with the specific zip codes that your buyers gave you in their criteria descriptions. Post in at least five different zip codes each morning and night. This expands your reach and network beyond your current reach. If you post only in one specific zip code, you will only reach so far. We want a BIG reach!

Now to the most important piece of your online ads, the ad copy! In other words, what should your ad say? Your advertisements should follow a very strict structure. You want them short, precise, to the point, and powerful! The structure of any good sales copy begins with hitting pain points. People listen when pain is involved. People can relate to the advertisement when you list a pain that they happen to be experiencing. Immediately after mentioning the pain, provide them with the solution. So, it looks something like this: Pain point > Solve the pain > Contact information to find out how. This will result in consistent calls and opportunities. Better yet, it will result in *free* consistent calls and opportunities. I love seeing the faces of people who do a deal and put $15,000 in their pocket using an ad that cost them exactly zero dollars and roughly 30 seconds of their time to post. You can do the math on that investment return. It's infinite!

Below is an exact ad that I post every single day. Notice that it is short and to the point and follows the structure explained above.

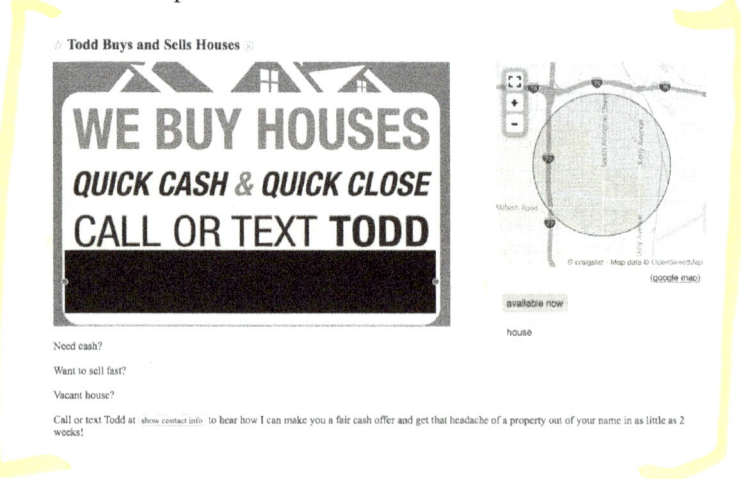

Todd Buys and Sells Houses

WE BUY HOUSES
QUICK CASH & QUICK CLOSE
CALL OR TEXT TODD

available now
house
(google map)

Need cash?
Want to sell fast?
Vacant house?

Call or text Todd at show contact info to hear how I can make you a fair cash offer and get that headache of a property out of your name in as little as 2 weeks!

As you can see, I have my logo with my name and contact on it (Sorry, you have to take me to dinner first to get my number!) so people get used to seeing my name, and I build a consistent brand. Notice in the ad copy that I list three pain points, and then immediately following that I list a plan to solve their problem, along with my contact information. You can mix up the pain points, using different reasons that people would want to sell. You don't have to keep the same three pain points every day. I have tried hundreds of combinations and absolutely nothing has beaten the structure of three pain points and a quick solution. I have tried listing one pain, five pains, ten pain points with a solution, and the number of calls and messages always dropped. In changing the structure and the length, I either don't touch enough people emotionally, or I begin to bore them with longer ads, and they move on before calling. Mimic my ad when creating yours, and I bet you the calls and messages will begin to roll in soon after.

I should mention that posting to Craigslist and finding the perfect storm is a bit of an art in itself. There are a lot of people on Craigslist, and anyone at any time can flag an ad for removal. Don't be discouraged if your ads are being removed when you first start. Some people don't like others trying to help, or they may even be other investors trying to eliminate their competitors' ads. Ignore this and stay consistent! You will outlast the people flagging your ads because, no matter what, you will be posting five to ten ads per day. The flaggers will eventually give up, and you will then own the market. That being said, I would like to point out that you should not remove other investors' ads. That is unethical and wrong. You shouldn't be deleting anyone's ads; you should be calling their ads and looking

4. **Local MeetUps – REIA (Real Estate Investors Association):** Hitting local networking groups allows you not only to network with buyers, but it also puts your ear to the ground and allows you to listen to possible problematic sellers with whom others are dealing. If someone else has a property under contract but has no buyer (because they aren't following this rule book!), there is an opportunity for you to step in with your buyer and get the deal closed. You guys can work together on the deal and split the profits. How cool is that?

5. **Local Courthouse – Pre-Foreclosure/Code Violation Leads:** The local county courthouse provides public records on foreclosure notifications, code violations, delinquent taxes, and property liens. These are hidden gems for you and your lead generation. These files and open violation records are all opportunities to solve seriously stressful problems. The pre-foreclosure files are especially useful because you have a seller who is being pressured by a multi-billion dollar corporation. This is potentially the most stressful moment of that person's life, and you can save him or her from it! The most important thing to understand when working with pre-foreclosures is the tight timeline that you are facing. You have only so much time before the property is sent to the auction block and the seller loses the house, eliminating the opportunity.

The best way to locate these files is to go physically into the courthouse and find either the fiscal office or the actual courtroom filing area, wherein you can ask the clerk or attendant how to locate the file on a specific foreclosure case. Sometimes this process can be a little more time consuming because some employees are less willing to help than others. Once again, it's important to remain level-headed and stay consistent. Return the following day and keep networking until you locate the correct case files. The more hoops you have to jump through to get the leads, the fewer the number of people who are going to do it. This will set you aside and put you in a class all by yourself. You will be the only one with eyes on these properties, and you will be able to capitalize on more opportunities.

The code violations can range from health hazards to lawn care. These are typically more difficult to locate than public record foreclosure cases, but, once again, finding them will put you in a league of your own.

To reach these sellers, you have a couple different options. You can send a piece of mail explaining that you purchase houses in the area in which the property is located. This is typically inefficient and will give you less time to work to solve their problem. The best thing you can do is to go knock on their door. Get in front of the person in pain and let them know that you purchase property in the area; let them decide if they want to have a conversation about selling. It's important that you don't come off as targeting these people, and this takes practice. Tell them you simply want to offer a solution to their problem, and leave it at that. It's important to check the laws and regulations within your state about foreclosure leads. Some states have different laws for foreclosure, so you need to be sure you are staying within the rules and regulations. Per usual, be ethical and honest.

6. **Driving For Dollars:** Driving for dollars is exactly like it sounds. You are driving around your market, or where your buyers are interested in purchasing property, and looking for distressed houses. You are looking for the tall grass and dilapidated siding. Anything that looks vacant or abandoned is an opportunity. These properties typically have other problems associated with them, which

can increase your leverage for negotiating. If the properties are sitting vacant, you can locate the seller through the county fiscal office real estate search website. Type in the address of the property in question, and you can pull up the public records for the property. Within these records will be a "tax mailing address." This is the address to which you should send a letter or flyer, informing the owner that you are interested in purchasing the property.

When you're able to reach the property owner, these can be very lucrative deals because the property is simply wasting away anyway, and the owners can be very reasonable when selling. If you aren't able to reach them via mailings, you can try using a private investigator or a skip trace service. These are usually very affordable, and they typically work relatively quickly. Before mailing or skip tracing, knock on a neighbor's door and ask them for contact information. This is often the best resource for finding an owner to a vacant property. It isn't uncommon for the neighbor to know the story of what's happened. Bottom line: if you see anything that looks out of order, mark the address down, and start asking questions!

7. **Flyers/Stickers Business Cards:** Telling everyone what you do is extremely important. To capitalize on this, you should have flyers and business cards handy at all times. These flyers can be handwritten or simply printed from your home computer if you have access to a printer. A batch of 500 business cards can be as little as $10 on sites like Vistaprint. You should be leaving business cards everywhere you go: on tables, barbershop stations, tack boards, local businesses, restaurants, gas stations, and anywhere else that has high traffic. The most important piece is to place these items in highly visible areas that have a large number of visitors. Gas pumps are great sources for this.

Everyone needs fuel for their car, and you can have a card or sticker ready and waiting to get your name out. Again, I don't want you to do anything illegal, so check to ensure you are allowed to advertise at any of these places before posting your flyer, sticker, or business card. I personally use cards that are the same as my logo on my online ads.

8. **Bandit Signs:** Using 18 x 24 inch signs is a great way to advertise what you do. These are referred to as "bandit signs" for a reason. They aren't always welcome. Many cities and ordinances don't allow this type of marketing in public areas; nevertheless, you see tons of them because they work. You can put your logo on these signs and place them around town on a Friday afternoon or night and pick them up on Sunday to avoid the city workers, but be aware that cities do hand out fines for using bandit signs excessively. A great way to do this legally is to place your signs in the yards of friends, loved ones, and fellow investor properties, with the owner's permission. This can get your name out without your having to worry about the signs being taken down. If you don't see many bandit signs in your area that state, "We buy houses," you should definitely consider using this type of marketing. You will be marketing in a way that others aren't, and you can capture a whole new lead type. Again, try to stay within legal regulations. Getting a fine in the beginning of your career won't sit well.

9. **Direct Mailing Campaigns:** Sending specific mailings to a filtered lead list is one of the most effective ways to get your name and brand in front of sellers at a consistent rate. The only real downfall of direct mailing is its cost. The average cost of a mailer is nearly 50 cents. So, if you send out hundreds or thousands of mailers a month, you will need to begin budgeting for this expense. This said, you don't need

to begin mailing until you try other free avenues first. Still, direct mailing can be a great tactic for scaling and growing. If you have the financial ability to mail from the outset, I highly recommend it. Direct mailing is my primary source of marketing and lead generation. Here is a picture of the letter that I use when mailing property owners:

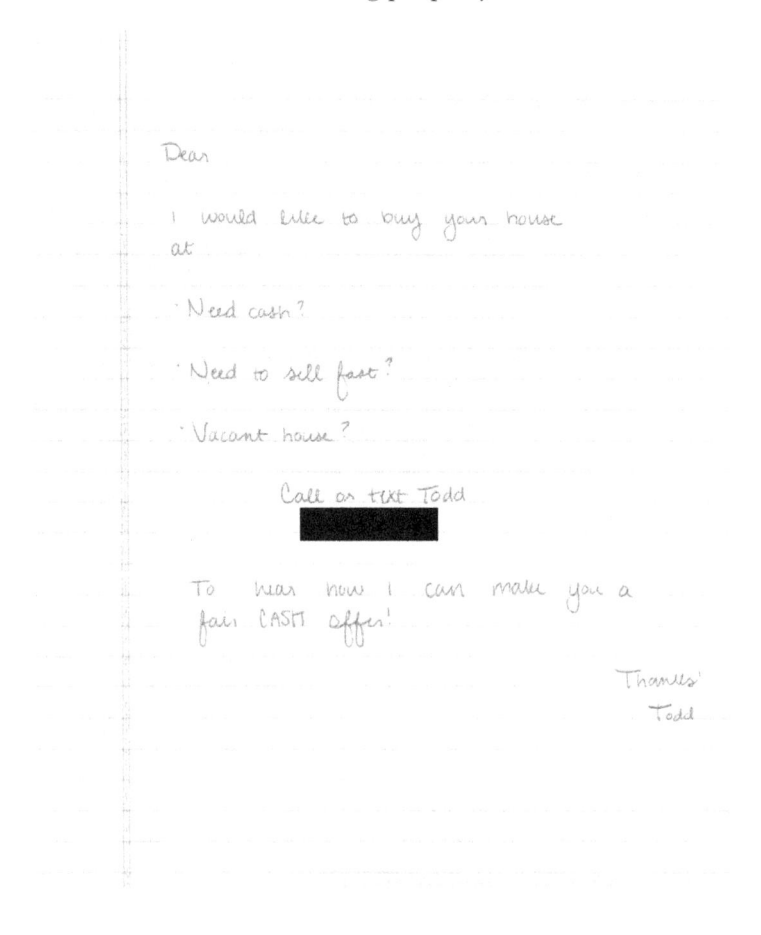

> Dear
>
> I would like to buy your house at
>
> · Need cash?
>
> · Need to sell fast?
>
> · Vacant house?
>
> Call or text Todd
> ███████████
>
> To hear how I can make you a fair CASH offer!
>
> Thanks
> Todd

I utilize the script and the structure of the above letter for all of my direct mailings. I stay true to the three pain points and the quick solution with contact information.

At the top, when greeting the owners, I use their first and last name. I make my letters as personable as possible while still making them quick and simple to read. This type of letter piques curiosity and will bring in a lot of calls. In my market I have received as high as 12-15% call-return rates. This means that when I send out 100 letters, I get up to 15 calls from that mailing. This return rate will differ among markets, but I can vouch that these are incredibly effective. I have tried all different types of letter structures, scripts, and lengths, and nothing has beaten the letter pictured.

Other details about the actual letter are important as well. I have tested different colors of inks and paper, along with different sizes of envelopes. The best results I have gotten are from using yellow notebook paper with red ink, mailed in a business-style envelope with no clear window, and with the name and address of the recipient written in red ink as well. I no longer place a return address on my envelopes. I have noticed that my returns drop a few percentage points if I do because it looks less personal.

Let's face facts. When we are mailing people directly, we are in the junk mail business. People sort their mail before they even make it back to their front door. We need to ensure that we make it inside. I do this by looking as much like a birthday card or invitation as possible. Whenever I include my return mailing address to a P.O. Box, people realize it isn't from someone they know. I have also taken notice of what junk mail I open at my house. I even have a running tally of what makes me open that piece of mail. What piques my curiosity and what deters me from opening it. This has allowed me to refine my own mailings and tweak them to the point where I can predict the number of calls that I am going to receive from each specific mailing.

In addition to nailing down a solid letter and envelope, you need to have a solid lead source to which you will mail your letter. If you can build your own customized list, you will know the information is accurate and up to date. The best site that I have found for building custom lists and having accurate information has been www.ListSource.com.

ListSource has a vast amount of information and options to scroll through and choose from. I could honestly take the next 50 pages explaining how to use the website and how to build each custom list from scratch, but it will be more effective for you to sit down and play with the website for 30 minutes. After just a few tries you will understand how to maneuver around the site and get a list started. I am going to give you a quick rundown on one of the many lists that I focus on, but if you want to learn more about specific custom lists and how to create them, visit www.thekingdomrealestate.com and consider becoming a family member! There are a multitude of training videos available on the website and within our community. As promised, here is a quick basic guide to one of my lists that I mail each week:

List Source Criteria: "Build List"

Geography > Zip Code > Specific zip codes of areas I love and in which my buyers love to purchase property

Skip Mortgage

Property > Equity (%) > 70-100%
Demographics > Household (Default)

Skip Foreclosure

Options > Absentee Owned > Exclude Corporate-Owned > Both Mailing and Property Address Complete

The above criteria will help narrow a search down to properties with substantial equity that are owned, which will help you drive down the purchasing price when there are problems with the property. This will also help you locate owners who don't live at the property, making it likely that there are problems to solve for the homeowner, who probably isn't emotionally attached to the property. This search has a greater chance of turning up properties that may be causing the owner pain due to vacancy or tenant problems. Overall, this results in a classic mailing list with the ability to pull a great return on calls.

You should mail to these lists more than once. If you mail an entire list three to four times, you will remain at the top of the owners' minds for a long time because you are the only investor who is following up in that area. I typically get more responses and deals closed from my second, third, and fourth mailings to a list than I do with the first mailing.

There are a lot of different mailing services and source sites from which to choose, but ListSource is my favorite. I won't mention any others from here on out. Instead, I will describe how these sites pull their information and organize their data. Each site can be different, but they still have to pull their property data from somewhere. They aren't magical sites that just suddenly know the newest homeowner and property information. These sites commonly pull from your local county websites and are able to access data and organize it in a way that saves you a massive amount of time. This is the source of their value: efficiency! It would take months to pull the data they are able to organize in a matter of seconds. That said, if you are tight on money and you want to build your own lists, you absolutely can. You can scale in one of two ways: time or money.

In the above section I have discussed just nine ways to market to possible sellers. There are literally hundreds of ways to get your name out into the marketplace. No matter how you choose to get your name out into the world, remember that the number one rule to marketing is consistency. You can't just place ads one time, or mail a list one time, and think it didn't work because you didn't get any calls. It takes time to build momentum. So remember: stay consistent!

GREAT QUESTION: AM I DOING AS MUCH AS I CAN AND BEING CONSISTENT IN MY MARKETING?

What To Expect From Sellers and Marketing Campaigns

Each type of marketing and each seller is different. Let's touch on what to expect from our marketing campaigns first. Each of the marketing techniques listed in the previous section are valuable in their own special way. Each one will also create different results and slightly different motivations from sellers. For example, an online ad is going to bring a higher rate of motivation from sellers than direct mailing. This is due to the fact that for them to find your ad on these sites, they already need to be looking for solutions. They are already looking for someone who might possibly buy their house. In contrast, when you do a direct mailing, you are soliciting hundreds and even thousands of people who may never think of selling a house in their life. This is why it is important to be running both types of campaigns. That way you can cover the entire market and not just one specific niche. Each market will also result in different returns for each marketing technique, but there is no way of knowing which way works best until you begin tracking your results. Get out there, start marketing, and adjust from there! If you have no money, start using all of the free methods first. It may take slightly longer to get a deal, but it will be 100% worth it once you realize you created money out of thin air.

In the beginning you can expect to be excited, scared, nervous, confused, and every emotion in between. The important point to remember is that it will get better. You will learn to control your emotions better day by day, and you won't have to worry about every second of the day like you do in the beginning. These new feelings are good! It means you are trying something new and outside of your comfort zone, which is the only place where real growth and success can occur.

When handling sellers and their emotions, you can expect a full range of conversations. These will range from highly motivated and needing an immediate solution to a nasty problem to tire-kicking, simply looking for a high sale price. You can also expect people to call and ask you what exactly it is that you do. Some people will find it odd that you are mailing them directly and will reach out simply to find out how you got their information. When this happens, keep the call quick and simple and just say, "We market to houses in the area because we love the area," and leave it at that. If you get drawn into a big discussion about how their property information is public record, it will just be a giant waste of time for you and them both. You will become skilled at moving calls along and determining motivations within 30 seconds of the start of the call. Naturally, at some point you will have a disgruntled caller who wants to give you their opinion of what you are doing. Simply say, "I appreciate your input, and if there is anything I can do to help in the future, let me know." And hang up. We aren't interested in the opinions of people who don't want help. Don't be discouraged the first time this happens. The best thing you can do is move on to that next call with someone who might need help. Have the mindset of "onto the next" lasered into your brain. Every successful investor and entrepreneur has to say that 100 times a day.

BIG QUESTION: AM I WORRIED ABOUT WHAT PEOPLE THINK, OR AM I WORKING ON CREATING WEALTH FOR MY FAMILY FOR GENERATIONS TO COME?

Seller Property Inspection

When you begin handling calls and asking great questions, you are going to begin unraveling some really awesome leads. When you build a solid relationship with a seller, it will be time to set an appointment and visit the property in discussion first hand. There are many different ways in which people go about looking at property. Some investors will only go look at a property if they already have it under contract and plan on renegotiating the purchase price later, but for right now I want you focused on getting in front of as many sellers as possible. I want you walking property and learning the skills of building rapport and asking great questions. The most important skill I want you to be practicing is listening! You can't get better at these things without getting in front of property owners and brainstorming how to solve their problems. So, for now, let's focus on getting appointments set up and walking through properties as more and more leads come in through our marketing campaigns.

Sellers are expecting you to want to see the properties and make them an offer. The perfect time to set proper expectations is when you are setting the appointment over the phone to look at a property. Let the seller know that you need to see the property to see how you can best help them. When you are setting the appointment, it is important that you control the conversation in the sense that you are leading them toward a specific time to come see the house. If you leave it up to the seller, it is likely that the meetup will never actually happen because the seller won't make a decision on when and where to meet. Let me give you an example: "Mr./Mrs. Seller, I can be at the property tomorrow at noon. How does that work for you?" This is a strong example of leading someone to a specific point.

In contrast, here is an example of a very weak question that can possibly lead to constant back and forth when trying to decide when to meet: "Mr./Mrs. Seller, if I were to come see the property sometime soon, when would you have time?" This question is entirely too open. It leaves the door open for responses such as, "I don't know," and, "Well, let me check my schedule and get back to you." This is a sign of weakness. Be strong and set the appointment. "Mr./Mrs. Seller, I have an opening in one hour before I hit two other houses in the area, so if you can meet me at the property to show me through, that would be perfect."

See the difference in confidence? Just reading those questions makes you feel differently about me. Use your language to your advantage.

Once the appointment is set, it's time to meet the seller. This is a nerve-racking time, but an exciting one at the same time. Before ever visiting a property, make sure you have asked the question, "Why do you want to sell?" This way you understand their motivation.

It's important that you stay safe while visiting property. If you are uncomfortable going alone, take someone with you. It's okay to do this. Let the seller know you may have a partner with you at the time, but that you will be at the meeting on time as planned. This will help keep you safe. Never enter a home or situation that causes you to fear for your safety. There are other opportunities and deals available–always. Don't put yourself in a bad situation because you were desperate for your first deal. Ninety-nine percent of the time, you won't have to worry about this, but I wanted to mention it in case you feel that something is off when you're first meeting with someone.

Meeting sellers is something that never gets old for me. I love meeting new people, and I love learning how I can help. My main focus when going into a home is to ask great questions, listen as much as possible, and take really good pictures for my potential buyers. I ask the seller if it's okay to take pictures of the property for my records, and I have never once had anyone take issue with it. They understand that certain actions need to be taken to sell the property. After listening to the seller talk about the property and why they want to sell, you can let the seller know how you plan to proceed. Transparency is immensely important. This is a great opportunity to let the seller know how the process works and what kind of time frame you will be working within if the two of you are able to strike an agreement.

Your relationship with your title group and the conversations you have had with your buyer give you a decent idea regarding how quickly everyone can close a deal that doesn't have any hidden issues. Let's use two weeks, or fourteen days, as an example of setting a time frame expectation:

"Mr./Mrs. Seller, I appreciate your showing me the property. I am excited to get going on this, but I just need to make sure we are on the same timetable. I understand you want to sell as quickly as possible, and I want to make sure we take care of that for you. We can typically close a deal in as little as two weeks. There are times when things can move a bit quicker, but once I get the deal over to the title group, we will be able to close as quickly as they can handle the paperwork with care."

Using similar dialogue sets the seller's expectations. The seller can't come back and say that you promised them you could close in three days now. If you were to leave this open-ended with a statement such as, "We can close faster than anyone," you would be leaving yourself vulnerable to serious communication issues. Make sure to use exact numbers/dates. You will later set this in ink on the purchase agreement, but for now you are verbally setting the timetable.

After the seller agrees to the timetable, you want to let him know that there are multiple ways in which this deal can close. It's important to explain all three possibilities so that the seller has a clear view of what your intentions are. This will earn you respect from your seller as well as build trust. Many times the seller will say that it doesn't matter, or that it's not necessary to explain everything, but they're wrong. It's important they know! Communication and transparency is key. This is the dialogue that I use, and I recommend you say something similar:

"Mr./Mrs. Seller, one of three things is going to happen here. I am going to close on the property myself, and keep it as a rental; I am going to close on the property myself and fix it up to resell it for a profit; or I am going to check with my partners, and if it fits one of their portfolios better, I will sell it to them, and they will step into my shoes at the closing table with you. No matter how we decide to close, I want you to know that you will get the exact dollar amount promised, and nothing will change on your end of the deal."

The above explains multiple aspects. One, it explains the possibilities for the closing. Two, it promises that their problem will be solved. Three, it announces that even though you are a problem solver first, you are running a business and will be making a profit on this property. This sets all expectations perfectly. The seller understands he will be out of the problematic property. He understands that you are serious that you will be making a profit regardless of which way you choose to close on the property. This is also perfect because it makes it easier to get the assignment form signed. You aren't just coming to your seller and surprising him with a new document stating you are making "X" amount on this property. This single tactic will ensure that your deals go smoothly, barring any issues out of your control.

This tactic will be revisited when we go over the contract signing portion of this book. This is because you will be restating these facts while signing any purchase agreement with a seller. This will remind them of the facts and will also help get the assignment sheet completed correctly.

Once we have stated the facts and set a solid timeline for the seller, it is time to say goodbye and move forward with the deal. You aren't signing anything with them at this point. You are letting the seller know that you are going to get with your partners ASAP and run some numbers to make them the best possible offer that you can. Let the seller know that you will call them in the next 24 to 48 hours.

DISCLAIMER: If you know for a fact this property is a screaming deal that won't last another few hours, I have no problem with your putting the property under contract to protect the deal as long as you know you have a buyer on the back end, ready to perform. If need be, excuse yourself from the seller for a moment and call your buyer while you are at the property. If they make an offer above the asking price, or the price at which you can purchase it, do the deal. Before signing any paperwork, make sure you review the contract and offer-making portion of this book to protect your interests and minimize risk!

GREAT QUESTION: MR./MRS. SELLER, HOW CAN I BEST SERVE YOU IN THIS CURRENT SITUATION?

STEP FOUR

Connecting With a Buyer After Locating a Deal

You left the seller's property. You are on your way home. You are excited. No, you're freaking out! This is fun, isn't it? It gets better, trust me! Let's hammer out how best to go about getting your buyers lined up and your first deal closed out.

Do your best to put your emotions aside so that you can begin to organize a plan. This is the point at which we match our buyer's criteria to the property that we just walked through. Mentally run through the handful of buyers and partners with whom you have a relationship and the confidence that they can perform on the deal at hand. I want you thinking about who fits this deal the best. If one of your partners is looking for 4 bedroom, 2 bath fix and flip deals, and this deal happens to be in a low-end neighborhood and has only 1 bedroom and 1 bathroom, this wouldn't be a great fit for that investor, would it? Now think of the investor who wants to buy and hold for passive income who happens to love small houses that are only a single floor. Perfect! That's the buyer you are going to be calling about the property you just walked through.

When you call the investor with a real possibility, the buyer will more than likely be happy to hear from you. You would be amazed at how many people fail to bring a single lead to a great buyer. Now that you have the possible buyer on the phone, explain that you just walked through a property within a specific neighborhood or zip code in which he or she likes to buy. Let him know that it fits his criteria for location and house type. At this point you will have piqued his interest, and you can let him know that you have great pictures that will give him a better idea of condition. The buyer may ask you your thoughts on the property or the specific situation, just as you did the seller. This is fine to relay. It's important to let the buyer know that you just walked through the property and that the seller is ready, but that you didn't want to put it under contract before speaking with him/her first. Ask the buyer what kind of price he or she would require in order to buy the property.

Notice I don't say, "Tell me what you could buy the property for and be able to pay me what I require for finding this deal." Your value is in negotiating great deals. If the buyer needs to be at $40,000 and you can only negotiate the price down to $36,000, then you are going to profit $4,000. You are not going to hold the property hostage by saying to the buyer, "The price is $36,000, and my minimum assignment fee is $10,000." At those numbers the property doesn't fit the buyer's criteria, and you are just trying to put more in your pocket than you have earned. Now, if the buyer needs to be at $40,000 and you are able to negotiate a great buy at $28,000, then you can sell the property to your end buyer for the agreed upon $40,000, or you can pass on some savings to your end buyer by selling it to him or her for $38,000 and absolutely solidify the fact that this buyer will be working with you in the future. That's powerful! That tactic of passing on savings to a partner will build massive business relationships that will surely pay you more than squeezing a couple more dollars out of a single deal ever will. ==Being ethical, honest, and transparent will build you a sustainable business to live on like no one else could have dreamed.==

Back to the deal at hand. You have notified a buyer of the property. You have shown him or her pictures and let him know why you think it is a good deal. You ask if he needs any more information. Below are some possible questions that the buyer might ask you. I provide some good answers to these questions to help you feel comfortable during this conversation.

Buyer: "How much does it need to be fixed?"

You: "I think it's best for you to look at it so that you can get a good estimate. Everyone has different prices, so I would hate to give you a bad estimate because I don't know your business as well as you do."

Buyer: "What are other houses in the area selling for?"

You: "I think its best you take a look at recent sales data that you are comfortable with so that we can both agree on a number that makes sense. There are so many ways to evaluate a property that I wouldn't want there to be a miscommunication."

Buyer: " What's the address of the property?"

You: "Again, I don't have the property under contract yet, but the property address is 123 Main."

DISCLAIMER: If you don't trust the buyer, you shouldn't be working with him in the first place. Giving him the property address so that he can do his due diligence shouldn't be an issue. Remind him or her that it is not under contract yet and that you are direct with the seller. If the buyer is a real investor he won't try to go behind your back and contact the seller for a cheaper price because he would be biting the hand that feeds. When you bring good deals to the table, he or she will want you to bring more!

Buyer: "I need to see the property in person. Can I do that?"

You: "Absolutely. I can set up a time with the seller. Just as a reminder, I don't have it under contract yet, so if you need me to have it under contract first, I can do that if you have an offer in mind. I would request that we don't talk numbers in front of the seller, though, to avoid any confusion."

Buyer: "Are you looking to wholesale this?"

You: "Yes, I prefer to assign the contract."

Notice how there is ZERO guessing by using this strategy. You will never have to guess a rehab value or a property value because the end buyer will be handling this for you. Once you become more experienced, you will be able to estimate these things quickly, but for now keep the conversation as fact-based as possible, with no guessing involved. This will be something that the buyer will thank you for in the end as well. He or she is either a solo investor or, more likely, a small team, and you can become a trusted part of the team when you show them this kind of value.

There are no formulas to use. There are no numbers to run. There is only good solid communication and transparency. When you act like you know everything and just blurt out numbers based on old formulas, you look like everyone else. You will fall into the pit of guessing and hoping your numbers match the investor's. Little spoiler: the numbers never match. Let the end buyer do his due diligence and work the best deal he knows. After all, you are partners!

GREAT QUESTION: IS THERE ANY OTHER INFORMATION THAT I CAN HELP FIND FOR YOU?

What Can You Pay?
"What would you need the price to be to make this a great deal for you?" The answer to this question will guide the rest of the process for this deal. If the buyer gives you a specific number that they would like, great! You now have a benchmark number to start working with when making an offer to your seller.

Many times this will be the situation. You will have provided a lot of valuable information, along with great pictures, on which to base a solid offering price. Sometimes there will be situations in which the buyer needs to see the property first hand to make a specific offer on the property. No problem! Some people begin to panic and think that the buyer is trying to go behind their back and negotiate the price themselves while cutting them out of the deal when the end buyer requests this. This isn't the case at all. The buyer just needs to do his or her due diligence and personally visit the property to make the best possible offer that he or she can.

When a buyer requests to see the property and walk through the house, simply remind him or her that the property is not yet under contract. Let the buyer know that if he requires the property to be under contract before visiting it, it's no problem and that you can get the property under contract first so that everyone's time is respected. But, you will need a ballpark offer number based on the information provided to take to the seller and negotiate a purchase price. At this point the buyer will more than likely give you a number, and you are once again set. You have a benchmark number to work with.

Occasionally, a buyer will not care whether or not the property is under contract, but just needs to see the property first before making any sort of offer. When this situation arises, follow the procedure outlined below:

1. Contact the seller and inform him or her that your partner needs to see the property before solidifying a final purchase offer.
2. Set an appointment with the seller and let your buyer know the best time to meet at the property so that all three of you will be together at the meeting.
3. Let the buyer know that when you arrive at the property so that he can do his walkthrough, you will stand with the owner at the front door.
4. When the buyer is finished walking the property, thank the seller for his/her time and let him know you will be in touch as soon as possible with an offer.
5. Contact the buyer and discuss the best possible number to make it a great deal for him.

See how simple that was! There was no reason to stress out, was there? Occasionally the house will even have a lockbox on the door, in which case you can just get the code from the seller and walk the property with your buyer and not worry about speaking with the seller separately. Either way, this is a simple process in which two partners are doing their due diligence before making an offer on a property. This is extremely common and won't be an outrageous request on your part. Many investors have partners, so don't worry about anyone feeling confused about why someone else would need to see the property.

After the buyer walks the property, he or she will have an offer for you. You are set! You now have a confident buyer who can perform on closing day and a number to set as a highest and best offer. When you reach this point, let the buyer know that you will be in touch asap to let them know if you can make that number work.

It's time to approach the seller with an offer and a solution to his problem!

GREAT QUESTION: AM I ENSURING MY BUYER GETS A GREAT DEAL, OR AM I WORRYING ABOUT MY CUT OF THE DEAL?

Step Five

Putting the Deal Together

It's nearly offer time! This is where we earn our keep. This is the step in which we provide options for solutions. We will be providing relief for whatever pain the seller is feeling. By focusing on this and being transparent we will ensure that we make the best possible offer for all parties involved. We will be enduring a lot of emotions and redirecting a lot of fear on our part. This is new to us! Remember, it's okay to be uncomfortable. After reading through this section, your nerves will be at ease, and you will know exactly how to navigate this portion of the deal. In the end, you are simply providing a solution. It is up to the seller to accept the relief or continue feeling the pain.

GREAT QUESTION: AM I FOCUSING ON PROBLEM SOLVING OR WORRYING ABOUT HOW MUCH I CAN MAKE ON THIS TRANSACTION?

Making the Offer

Rule number 1: you make offers in person. You do not text offers. At the very least, you will make the offer over the phone, but if you can avoid this and make the offer in person, your success rate will skyrocket. Making the offer in person is more professional and more personal. The seller will be able to see that you care and that you are looking to help in any way possible. Remember that rapport building? Remember how you actually care for your sellers? This makes a big difference when the offer is coming from a real person and not just the screen on a phone. I understand that there are times in which the offer needs to be made over the phone, but if you can, meet with the seller in person.

When delivering the purchase offer in person, you will want to prepare your offer for the seller so that it is simple to understand. Many people will just show up a with a number and a face that says, "Yeah? Is that good enough?" We are going to be more prepared than that. We are going to have a purchase agreement contract with us and an assignment sheet ready so that we can have both signed at once. We are going to meet either at the property or in a public venue in most cases. This will allow us a few minutes to not only make our offer, but to explain how we derived the numbers. We will be able to demonstrate that we didn't just pull a number out of thin air. This will provide validity. This is a good thing.

When beginning to make the offer, start with the facts first: "We love the property, and to get it into top condition we need to do this, this, and this, which will cost a certain amount." This will begin to explain why your number is going to be what it is. You can use other recently sold prices in the area to show what the property will be worth when it's fixed up. Be transparent on what you will be making for so many months of your time and work. Overall, the biggest focal point needs to be the problem you are solving. For example, "Mr./Mrs. Seller, I feel this offer is good to get you moved into a new apartment," or, "Mr./Mrs. Seller, I feel like this offer is perfect to help pay off those debts and assure you that you won't have any more costs associated with this property."

It's important to remind the seller of the pain point that you have been focused on relieving. If you fail to do this, it can become a purely transactional situation, where the only thing that matters is the number. When there is a large problem to solve, numbers no longer matter as much. The pain being healed is much more important.

At this point you have explained why your offer is what it is, and you present your offer. Whether the seller accepts your offer is up to him or her, but what's important is that you are getting your offer number below where your buyer needs to be. For example, let's say your buyer has agreed to pay $40,000 for the property. This being the case, you will go to the seller and offer the seller $30,000 for the property, so at closing the seller will get $30,000, and you will receive $10,000 for your services and problem-solving skills. As you improve your negotiating skills, you will increase your spreads and profits. There is a saying I was taught by a mentor of mine that I love: "You do your first couple deals to learn; you do the ones after that for profit." Later on in this book there will be a section dedicated to increasing profits and thinking outside the traditional perspective of cash-only wholesale deals.

If the seller rejects your first offer, that's perfectly okay. The conversation is now open, and you know the absolute maximum number you can pay. If the seller is comfortable anywhere below that number, you have a deal! It's important to remember your value in this transaction. You have earned a profit. You have provided a value to your buyer, but more importantly, you are providing a huge solution to your seller. If need be, remind the seller that there is no solution above a certain price point. Which is worse? A couple thousand dollars or being stuck in the same situation?

GREAT QUESTION: HOW CAN I PROVIDE THE MOST VALUE TO MY SELLER WHILE STILL MAKING THE DEAL WORK?

Contract Signing
If and when the seller accepts an offer below your buyer's offer, you will have your first deal to structure and sign off on. You will have the purchase agreement with you as well as the assignment sheet, as discussed. The purchase agreement contract can be simple. It can be your state's contract, or it can be a contract that was sent to you by your title group/attorney. It doesn't need to be a 50-page contract, which can make the seller uncomfortable. You are going to read through the agreement with the seller, and you will fill out everything in front of them. If the seller has questions, you need to address them as best as you can. If you don't know an answer to a question, it's okay to let them know that you aren't 100% sure, but that you can find out from the title group/attorney before moving any further. It's important that everyone is on the same page.

NEVER FORGET

NEVER FORGET TO PROTECT YOURSELF IN THE CONTRACT! DO NOT FORGET TO PUT VERBIAGE IN THE CONTRACT THAT STATES THAT YOUR OFFER IS DEPENDENT ON A PARTNER'S APPROVAL. THIS PROTECTS YOU IF THE END BUYER WERE TO BACK OUT FOR SOME REASON. YOU WOULD NO LONGER HAVE A PARTNER'S APPROVAL AND COULD THEN EXIT THE CONTRACT LEGALLY WITHOUT ISSUE. OTHER CONTINGENCIES INCLUDE INSPECTION TIMES AND TITLE SEARCHES. IF IT IS NOT ALREADY IN THE CONTRACT, WRITE THIS EXACT SENTENCE:

"THIS OFFER IS CONTINGENT UPON THE APPROVAL OF A PARTNER, AS WELL AS AN INSPECTION PERIOD UP UNTIL THE CLOSING DATE."

THIS IS PERFECTLY FAIR TO HAVE IN THE CONTRACT. ALMOST ALL REAL ESTATE TRANSACTIONS HAVE SOME SORT OF PROTECTION FOR EACH PARTY INVOLVED. YOU NEED TO MAKE SURE THAT YOU HAVE AT LEAST ONE LEGAL OUT IN CASE THINGS GO WRONG FOR SOME REASON.

After ensuring you're protected and filling out the purchase agreement with the agreed-upon offer price, you are going to move to the assignment sheet. The assignment sheet is extremely simple and only needs to be a few lines. (We provide contracts and assignment sheets within The Kingdom Real Estate if you have trouble locating any. Head over to www.thekingdomrealestate.com and sign up for any of the memberships to gain access to them.) The assignment sheet will explain that Party A (Seller) and Party B (You-Wholesaler) have agreed to a purchase price on a specific property address. Directly following is a statement that Party B (You-Wholesaler) assigns original purchase agreement between Party A (Seller) and Party B (You–Wholesaler) to a 3rd party, Party C (End Buyer) for X amount of dollars as an assignment fee. Both you and the seller sign at the bottom of the assignment sheet. You now have your first executed contract between you and a seller. Congratulations! It's time to get it signed by the buyer now.

Thank the seller for his time and patience and reiterate what the general timeline of the deal looks like. You will be in contact with the seller frequently after this point to continue setting expectations, but, for now, you will be focusing on finalizing signatures on the buying end.

GREAT QUESTION: DOES THE SELLER UNDERSTAND 100% OF THE SALES CONTRACT?

Signing With the End Buyer (Assignment)
This part is nice and simple. Contact the end buyer and let him/her know that you have an executed contract with the seller and that his offer of "X" dollars will work out just fine. You can either meet up with the buyer that day or send him the paperwork online. You will be sending him the original purchase agreement between you and the seller and the completed assignment sheet

with all of the disclosed numbers on it. At this point the buyer will sign the assignment sheet and return it to you. You will now have a completed signed purchase agreement between you and the seller and a completed signed assignment sheet between you, the seller, and the end buyer. That's it for this piece! Double check with your buyer and make sure he/she is ready to perform in the allotted amount of time, and then get ready to send your executed contracts to the title group or closing attorney.

Signing With the End Buyer (A-B-C Close/ Double Close)

If for some reason you cannot complete an assignment of contract, you need to get organized so that you can perform an A-B-C closing. Instead of sending the end buyer your original contract with the seller and a completed assignment sheet, you will be sending him/her a completed purchase agreement between you and him/her (end buyer) with his/her offer price as the purchase price. You will have separate purchase agreements between you and the seller and you and the end buyer. For example, the original contract between seller and you is for $32,000, and the contract between you and your end buyer is for $40,000, leaving you a profit of $8,000 before any fees and costs associated with closing. This part isn't overly complicated, but you will certainly walk away with less than you would have by assigning the contract with the same numbers. However, my goal is for you to be knowledgeable about all scenarios, not just one.

GREAT QUESTION: HAVE I SET THE SAME EXPECTATIONS FOR THE SELLER AND THE BUYER?

Step Six

Contacting the Closing Agent

Regardless of whether you are closing with a single attorney or a title group, the information in this section remains the same. You will be setting expectations and explaining the details of the transaction in full while sending the attorney/title group the appropriate signed paperwork. What you need to send under the different types of closings is as follows:

Assignment of Contract: Original purchase agreement between you and seller, assignment sheet signed by you, the seller, and the end buyer. You will also need to send names and contact information for yourself, the seller, and the buyer so that the title group can contact everyone as necessary.

A-B-C Close: Original contract between you and seller, separate purchase contract between you and the end buyer. Along with the purchase contracts, you will need to send over transactional funding contracts/paperwork if you do not have the funds to close on the first deal yourself. Don't forget to provide the contact information for everyone involved, including you, the seller, the buyer, and the transactional funding company. The paperwork for the transactional funding will be provided by the company that you choose to fund the first part of the deal, so don't stress out about not having specific paperwork for it at this point in time.

After sending the completed documents to the closing agent, you will want to be in contact with them and let them know your plan of attack on this specific transaction. If assigning, you will let the agent know that you are assigning the original purchase contract to the end buyer and that the end buyer will be stepping into your shoes at closing. The agent will understand what to do from there.

It is a slightly more complicated conversation when dealing with a double closing. You will explain to the closing agent that you will be completing two clean buy and sell transactions. The first transaction with the attached paperwork is the one in which you buy the property from the original seller. The second transaction will be the sale of the property by you to your end buyer. Note that you will be paying two sets of closing costs and insurances during this type of transaction because you are technically purchasing the property and then immediately reselling it. You will also be on the chain of title for this property forever.

The most important aspect when contacting the closing agent is to be clear in your language and communication. When problems arise, it is usually because of poor communication, and someone misunderstood something along the way. Again, these deals aren't nearly as common as most, so it is best to be dealing with someone who has dealt with these types of transactions in the past. If you can, speak with each team member at the title group and introduce yourself. This will help build rapport, and it will help the title group team members understand what is going on. I like to let them know that they can call me at anytime when they have a question. It's much better to receive 10 calls with questions before closing than to have someone make a guess about something because he/she isn't comfortable enough with you to call.

You have come to the point now where it is a waiting game. In the next section we are going to cover setting expectations with your seller as well as your buyer.

GREAT QUESTION: DOES EVERYONE UNDERSTAND THAT THEY CAN REACH OUT TO ME AT ANYTIME WHEN THERE IS A QUESTION?

Step Seven

What To Expect

At this point we now have our first transaction set up and waiting to close. This is also about the time that you will begin getting really nervous and fearing the worst. This is natural. Don't worry about being nervous and excited at the same time. The best thing you can do during this time is to go find another deal. You want your sales pipeline full at all times. I myself have been guilty of sitting and waiting for a deal to close, letting more opportunity pass me by day by day. My best advice is to keep moving!

In addition to moving on your next lead and opportunity, you need to stay in contact with everyone involved in your first deal, which is now at the title company, being organized for closing. First off, let the seller know that the ball is rolling and that closing will be coming up shortly. Let the buyer know that the paperwork has been submitted and to be ready for closing when the time comes. Lastly, be sure to stay in contact with the title group every few days and monitor the progress. This will help keep the lines of communication open should any title issues

Immediately following the closing, I like to reach out to my seller and make sure that he or she is totally satisfied. This is important because he/she is going to be a growing piece in your network. He will be a great tool for referrals and testimonials. I keep all records of my sales and the contact information of everyone I do business with. You will thank me for this piece of advice when one sale turns into multiple deals.

Following up with the buyer is also important. You need to find more property for him or her, right? Ask questions about how the property is working out for him and what kind of costs he had to bear to fix it up if the property needed anything. This will be valuable information to you as you learn how to estimate repair costs and get better at serving your buyer. When you know what the property was like and then you get a rehab number later on, you can relate that to future projects and opportunities.

Lastly, get back in touch with your closing agent and title team. Thank them for all of their hard work and taking care of you. Let them know you are excited to do business with them again. This will be an important factor in growing your team. They will want to work with you more and do better and faster work for you in the future.

GREAT QUESTION: HOW CAN I BRING EVEN MORE VALUE TO MY PARTNERS ON MY NEXT CLOSING?

Step Eight

Repeat the Process

Sounds simple enough, right? Well, it wouldn't be a step in the process if it was that easy. There is some fear in repeating the process, actually. We have learned a lot about the markets and how to build relationships. We have closed our first deal. But what if we can't do it again? That's the killer question! That's the question that sends us back to Square One and keeps us from taking action again. Don't let this happen to you! Don't allow your mindset to shift back to the "what if" state of scarcity. If it does, instead of asking yourself, "What if I can't?" simply ask yourself "**What if I can?**"

An action step that will help you in repeating and refining your process is to look back at your first deal and how it came to be. How did your seller find you? How did you market? Were you consistent in your marketing? How did you locate the buyer who was able to perform at closing? Can you work with that specific buyer again? How long did it take you to close your first deal? How many deals fell through before you closed your first? How many leads did it take before you made an offer that was accepted? What was the motivation of the seller in that particular closing?

When you answer all of these questions, you will be able to look at your business and refine the model in which you are building. If it took four months to close your first deal, but you weren't marketing consistently, you know that you can cut down on that time. You now know where to market. You know who to market to. You know who is going to buy a deal like this. You know how to negotiate the future deal. You have learned how to keep your emotions in check and your action up. You also have the relationships in place to do another deal today, as opposed to in a few weeks. Once you do your first deal, the red carpet rolls out. There is a mindset shift, and the thought, *This is possible* changes to, *This is real!* That shift alone will allow you to do your next deal faster than you did your first. After your second comes your third. After you close your third, you will already have your fourth in the pipeline and on its way. This is what's so beautiful about this game. Your knowledge and experience will begin to grow, and you will no longer be starting at Square One over and over when you take consistent, faithful action!

GREAT QUESTION: WHAT IF I CAN?

Step Nine

Bonus Step
What No One Else is Telling You About Wholesaling

This is a special bonus that I wanted to share with you. The following couple of tactics are rarely discussed, and even more rarely practiced. The amazing part about this section is that this is where you derive the real profits in wholesaling. This is how you can be paid hundreds of times for completing just a single deal! Why wouldn't people talk about this more? Is this meant to be a secret? Is this too complicated to understand without years of training? Absolutely not. These tactics aren't typically taught because they aren't known. People tend to learn how to do something one way and then stop learning about how to grow in the same space. I don't want that to happen to you! Read on if you want to learn how to double and triple your profits and turn $10,000 wholesale transactions into $20,000 with multiple payouts.

GREAT QUESTION: AM I SEEING ALL OF THE OPPORTUNITES AVAILABLE TO ME, OR HAVE I STOPPED LEARNING ABOUT MY INDUSTRY?

Wholesaling to Retail Buyers

Throughout this book I have discussed step-by-step strategies for locating problems, helping sellers out of bad situations, and selling your interest in property to investors who are your end buyers. Now, when you sell to an investor, the property would typically need to be at a great discount to them in order for the deal to make sense on both ends. What if you could sell your interest in property to non-investors? What if you could sell your properties to retail buyers who are actively looking for a home to live in? Wouldn't the profits be much greater? Let's look at an example using numbers:

Typical wholesale transaction: Property is worth $100,000, finished and cleaned up. You have the property under contract for $45,000, and you sell it to your investing partner for $50,000 since, at the time of the sale, the property needs $20,000 in repairs. This leaves the end buyer with $30,000 profit when he or she resells the property to a retail buyer who is going to live in the home. The seller had a problem solved. You made $5,000, and the investing partner made $30,000 in this scenario.

Now let's look at a scenario in which you sell your interest in this $100,000 property to the retail buyer:

Retail Buyer Wholesale Transaction: Property is worth $100,000, finished and cleaned up. You have the property under contract for $45,000, and you have a retail buyer who may be interested in the property. You let the retail buyer know that they can fix up the property however they wish and that it will cost roughly $20,000 to do so. You let the retail buyer know that you will sell them the property and your interest for $75,000, which will leave them enough for closing costs and some wiggle room in their rehab. At the end of the rehab, they will have their dream home within their $100,000 budget. They agree to purchase your interest in the property, and they take ownership of the home for $75,000. Let's look at the numbers a little closer. You just sold your interest for THE EXACT same property in the exact same condition without any extra work for an extra $25,000!

Wholesale profit to investing buyer - $5,000
Wholesale profit to retail end buyer - $30,000

Too good to be true? Wrong! This type of transaction is what the most successful investors look for. Successful investors look to solve the biggest problems and structure the deals to be the most profitable for their business. In my own personal business, my largest profits have come from end buyers who plan to live in the property after closing. They have equity in the home the instant they buy from you and have the ability to do what they wish. This is a win-win!

Would you rather sell your interest in one property or six in order to attain the same level of profit? How much more effective would your business be if each of your wholesale transactions doubled, tripled, and quadrupled in bottom-line profits? I hope you're as excited as I am about this because this took me years to discover! I endured endless headaches before I discovered how to structure these deals in a way that would work for everyone involved. Now you have this extra tool in your tool belt to continue to grow in your business without any extra effort or time. Leveraging this knowledge and practicing this new skill will grow your business ten times faster than if you sell only to cash-buying investors. Those who do so are limiting themselves in their potential.

Now that we understand that anyone on this planet looking for a house to purchase can be your end buyer, how do we structure this deal? The deal is structured in the exact same fashion as previously discussed in this book. You simply plug in the retail buyer instead of an investor as your end buyer. You will disclose everything in the same fashion as well. Nothing changes if the retail buyer is using cash or capital that he/she has readily available to close on the property via assignment or double close.

What if the end buyer needs to get a loan for the property, Todd? No problem! No worries here, either. You can assign a contract to anyone. So, this shouldn't be an issue for you or the end buyer. That being said, if the retail buyer is getting a loan from a traditional bank, the due diligence period in your original contract with the seller will need to cover this timetable. Typical loans take 30 to 45 days to be funded and closed. If your contract with the original seller is for 10 days, that obviously won't work. In that case, simply go back to your original seller and let them know you and your partner have decided to get a loan to fund the deal on the property and that your due diligence period will need to be extended to accommodate the fact that it typically takes 30 to 45 days for the bank's funds to reach the closing table.

In addition to ensuring the due diligence period is sufficient, you will also need to make sure that the property will stand up to any inspections that the bank requires for lending. For example, if the end buyer is getting an FHA loan (one of many loan types offered by banks), be aware that this type of loan isn't available on properties that require major rehabs, so the property under contract would need to be in good condition as-is for this type of deal to work. If the end buyer is getting a traditional loan with less stringent rules and regulations for approval, then you won't have to worry about this as much. Bottom line: this isn't something to get stuck on. Simply disclose that the funding partner requires a few inspections to your seller and tell him or her that you will be in touch to schedule these at no cost to him/her. Have the inspections completed and then move forward with the deal as planned.

Again, you can assign a contract to anyone looking to buy, so don't limit yourself to only cash-buying investors. This being said, you will need to assign contracts to retail buyers getting a loan. If for some reason you need to double close, it is not as simple a deal to sell to retail buyers. The banks typically won't loan on deals in which you are not on the title as the seller. In this case, you would need to close on the property yourself and then begin the process of selling the property to your end buyer, so you would own the property for 30 to 45 days. You can still fund this type of transaction with money other than your own, but it is not as readily available. You will need to have private money or hard money in place to complete this type of transaction, but that is a discussion for another book. Just know that you should be focusing on assigning contracts in these cases, but that, as a last resort, it is possible to close on the property and then resell it later down the road.

GREAT QUESTION: AM I MAKING MYSELF AVAILABLE TO EVERYONE LOOKING TO BUY A HOUSE THIS YEAR?

Building Passive Income Through Wholesaling

Passive income is the income that comes to you whether you work for it or not. An example of passive income is the income that is generated when you own a rental property or a business. Whether you go to work that day or not, you get paid. This is the key to building financial wealth in life. The greater the passive income you can build, the freer you will become.

Actually, passive income is a topic for a future book, but I needed to give a quick explanation of it so that you understand why passive income is so powerful. Wouldn't it be nice to get paid hundreds of times for doing a job one single time? Well, guess what? You can do this wholesaling! You can build passive income and be paid for years after doing a single deal. So, how do we go about doing this? We change the structure of the payments from our end buyer. Instead of receiving one lump sum up front as an assignment fee, we request a promissory note from the end buyer.

A promissory note is a promise to pay a certain amount over a specific amount of time. For example, you may hold a promissory note for $10,000, with the terms that you will be paid $200 per month for 50 months by the end buyer. This increases your passive income each month by $200. Notice that this example didn't have any interest involved. When accepting a promissory note as opposed to a fee up front, it can also make sense to add interest to the payments because you are providing a service. The end buyer doesn't have to come up with a large up-front payment, so it's easier for the end buyer to do the deal.

For example, that same promissory note for $10,000 might have a 10% interest rate tacked on, which would increase your monthly income payment to $245.37 per month and your end profit from $10,000 to $12,268.61. You would earn over $2,000 in interest paid directly to you for providing creative options to your end buyer. This is how you build wealth! This is how you maximize your profits!

The first few deals you structure this way more than likely won't change your life because it will only be a couple hundred dollars per month, depending on the size of the note, but when you repeat this process multiple times, you will find yourself financially free, with more passive income than expenses per month. This is what will change your lifestyle forever! Structuring this type of deal is also simple, so let's cover that quickly.

The great part about having awesome team members for closing, such as title groups or closing attorneys, is that we don't have to handle all the paperwork and details for these small adjustments at closing. When you reach an agreement with an end buyer to accept a promissory note in lieu of an upfront fee, you simply contact the title group or attorney and send them the details of the note and agreed-upon terms, such as $10,000 with 10% interest to be paid monthly over 50 months in installments of $245.37. At this point the closing agents will draw up a promissory note agreement for you and the end buyer to sign. At closing, instead of paying an assignment fee along with the purchase price of the home, the end buyer will only pay the purchase price of the home. You will start to receive payments the following month from your end buyer, as specified in the terms of the note.

An important aspect of this type of transaction is that you will be protected. You will not have to worry about whether or not you will be paid because you will now hold a security lien position on this property, just as a bank holds a lien on your property when you get a loan. The bank can foreclose on you and take the property back if you don't pay. You now have this security as a lien holder on the property. If, for whatever reason, the buyer stops paying you, you can take legal action.

When the end buyer is purchasing the property with cash, you will hold what's called a first lien position. This means that if the property is sold before your note is satisfied, you will be paid first. Your lien position has to be cleared before the title can transfer hands again. This is your security. If the end buyer happens to have a loan in place to fund the deal, you will most likely be in second position. This is a less secure position technically because if the property has no equity and has to be sold, the holder of the first lien (the bank) will be paid before you will be paid anything. If there is nothing left after the bank's lien is satisfied, you will receive nothing. This is the small risk you face in this type of scenario. I don't recommend that you take positions beyond second lien position for this reason.

GREAT QUESTION: AM I FOCUSING ON BUILDING MY WEALTH THROUGH PASSIVE INCOME?

Wrap Up

You now have the knowledge and the tools to complete your first deal in real estate with absolutely no previous experience or money of your own. The only things holding you back at this point are your excuses and lack of action. Massive action is the only thing that will get you your first deal. All of the knowledge and experience shared in this book will be completely useless unless you go out and take the action described in each of these steps. It pains me to say this, but I hate it when I see someone so capable of great things sit on the sidelines due to fear and feeling uncomfortable. This is why I included so much on mindset in the first half of this book. If you feel unable to take that action step, re-read the first half of this book and immediately post a free online ad or make a call to a title group. Do something. Anything! This one step will help build your confidence, and one step will turn into many great steps toward your future success.

GREAT QUESTION: AM I TAKING ACTION?

In Closing

My greatest motivation for writing this book is to give you the mental foundation needed to start building your wealth and your financial freedom. In my opinion, everyone needs to strive for financial freedom so that he or she can focus on what he/she loves in life. Everyone has the ability to follow his desires and his heart so that he can make an impact on the world in the best way possible. By providing a step-by-step process for you to complete your first risk-free deal, I hope to move you past the research phase and into the action phase. Taking action is the only way to reach your greatest goals and achieve your biggest successes.

GREAT QUESTION: IS THE FEAR THAT'S HOLDING ME BACK COVERED IN THIS BOOK?

About The Author

Todd Fleming currently spends his time investing in real estate and teaching others how to do so within The Kingdom Real Estate. Todd also spends time teaching financial strategy within his Facebook group called "Power Of Finance With Todd Fleming." You can also sign up for his financial freedom newsletter at www.PowerOfFinance.com. When not investing and teaching, he enjoys spending time with his wife Denise, son Wyatt, and dog Gracie. He is an avid reader and reads a book a week about business, finance, mindset, and self-awareness. He also loves video games and has plans to share his love of gaming on his live streaming account at www.Twitch.Tv/Toddshi. Here Todd shares his love of gaming while talking about his love of finance, business, real estate, and relationships. Todd credits his success in business and finance to the relationships that he has built over the years. He states, "Nothing would be possible without the amazing partners and friendships that I have been so fortunate to have in my life." Todd has shown the ability to adapt and learn while being creative enough to complete his first wholesale transaction with only $11 in his checking account. This alone proves that when the mind focuses on a certain goal and completely banishes any thought of quitting, anyone can be successful in achieving the goal. Todd is a firm believer that the most important thing in life is that you follow your desires. Your desires will lead you to happiness, which is the true goal in everyone's lives.

GREAT QUESTION: AM I FOLLOWING MY HEART AND MY DESIRES?

Want to Work with Todd Personally?

Join the Kingdom Real Estate and get personal coaching to achieve your wildest dreams: **WWW.THEKINGDOMREALESTATE.COM**

Recommended Media

GET FURTHER COACHING FOR FREE WITH THE KINGDOM PODCAST ON ITUNES AND STITCHER

Top 5 recommended books by Todd

1. The Richest Man In Babylon – George S Clason
2. You are Born Rich – Bob Proctor
3. You are a Bad Ass at Making Money – Jen Sincero
4. The Third Circle Theory – Pejman Ghadimi
5. The Go Giver – Bob Burg and John David Mann

Download free guides and case studies from our website at www.thekingdomrealestate.com

Learn how to make and keep more money at www.PowerOfFinance.com

UPCOMING BOOKS

This book is just part 1 of a 3-book series. Make sure to keep an eye out and sign up for our newsletter to get alerts, updates, and free tips and tricks before the next book comes out at www.thekingdomrealestate.com

Acknowledgements and Testimonials

Benjamin - First off, I am so thankful that Todd thought of me to be part of the first group of people to read his new book. Todd is an amazing person and I'm lucky enough to be learning so much from him, but by far the greatest pleasure of working with Todd is the friendship that has developed out of our mutual love for real estate and video games.

I'm a lot like Todd was back in the day with 11 dollars to his name. I've tried and failed many things and I too decided that real estate is what's going to cement my name in history and ensure my family and friends are taken care of forever.

Todd's book doesn't pull any punches. He does an excellent job of explaining the wholesale process in a way that is easy to understand and Todd shows you exactly what you need to do to be successful when you are starting from nothing.

I've been taking the action set out in this book and I have no doubts that I will do a deal if I stick with what Todd is teaching in this book. The only thing more exciting that getting a sneak peek at the book will be getting a physical copy I can mark up and reference on my journey.

Thank you Todd for focusing your time on others and putting your knowledge into this book. This will undoubtedly change your life if you take the action and put away your fears. It's not easy, but I know it is worth it.

Brandon - This book is exactly what is needed for anybody looking to get started in real estate investing. Todd does such a great job of simplifying complex concepts. He takes all the guess work out of it and makes a step by step system that anybody can follow. Learning from his mistakes and his years of trial and error to figure out what works so that we don't have to. That way you can feel comfortable and confident when you finally take the leap into real estate investing. You can feel the passion he has for this industry and how much he wants to help solve problems and get people financially free. That's why he starts with and insists that we change our mindset and become financially educated. I have no doubt that anyone that follows the contents within this book will soon see themselves out of the rat race.

Ashley - This book is so jam packed full of information it will require you to read it twice. It's a very easy read and direct to the point that if you use this information you will be successful in real estate. There are pages full of marketing ideas, mindset, and role play scenarios. Even though this book is mostly about starting off in real estate by wholesaling the information is foundational to many other aspects of the real estate business. Mr. Fleming's life story is paramount to show that anyone with zero money or experience can make it with determination. He's put all the right steps into a simple step by step guide so you won't have to make all the mistakes yourself, so this is a must read.

Brett - Having recently joined The Kingdom I have to say I was beyond excited when Todd selected me to read his wholesaling book. Especially given the fact I had not done my first wholesale deal yet. Reading this has made me even more excited about real estate than ever before and I can't wait to take action and get my first deal (and many more) done. The first half of the book on mindset had me completely addicted and I had to just read more and more. The second half of the book gave me everything I needed to get deals done and learn even more of what I needed. I just needed to have more of this knowledge and continued reading as my excitement built. By the end of the book I was left thinking "that's it? It really is that easy?" and from there contacted nearly 10 buyers today and less than an hour ago spoke to someone in my home state who is willing to mentor me and wants me to put him as the "#1 buyer on my list" of people who I call as he said he can close deals fast and has lots of cash available! We are meeting next week to get lunch along with a second buyer I spoke to. This stuff really works and by the time this book is published I'm certain I'll have multiple deals to add into this testimonial!

Made in the USA
Monee, IL
31 July 2021